DOMINIC BLISS is the former editor of men's wedding
magazine *Stag & Groom* and writes for many British magazines
including *Wedding Directory* and *Bridal Buyer*. Married with
two kids, he has attended almost as many friends' weddings
as he's had birthdays.

This reformatted edition published in 2012 by New Holland Publishers (UK) Ltd.
First published in 2005 by New Holland Publishers (UK) Ltd
London · Cape Town · Sydney · Auckland
www.newhollandpublishers.com

Garfield House, 86–88 Edgware Road, London W2 2EA, United Kingdom
80 McKenzie Street, Cape Town 8001, South Africa
Unit 1, 66 Gibbes Street, Chatswood, NSW 2067, Australia
218 Lake Road, Northcote, Auckland, New Zealand

10 9 8 7 6 5 4 3 2 1

A catalogue record for this book is available from the British Library

ISBN 978 1 78009 136 5 (print)
ISBN 978 1 78009 138 9 (Pdf)
ISBN 978 1 78009 137 2 (ePub)

Publisher: Aruna Vasudevan
Senior Editor: Jolyon Goddard
Editor: Wendy Horobin
Editorial Assistant: James Caven
Design: 2m design
Cover Design: Celeste Vlok
Production: Kylie Rodier
Printer: Toppan Leefung Printing Limited (China)

Note: The author and publishers have made every effort to ensure that all
information given in this book is safe and accurate, but they cannot accept
liability for any resulting injury or loss or damage to either property or person,
whether direct or consequential and howsoever arising.

BEST MAN
BEST SPEECH

How to be the
best best man

Dominic Bliss

CONTENTS

Introduction

Are you feeling like you might have bitten off more than you can chew? It's a serious responsibility being best man. There's a lot to do, a lot to remember and, of course, during the speech, a lot to say.

You'll be pleased to know that you don't have to embark on your new duties completely alone. The in-depth advice you'll find in this book will make your task much easier. Follow my step-by-step advice and, with a bit of luck, everything will go swimmingly. The book is divided into two parts – Part One deals with everything except the speech, from your appointment as best man to the wedding day, and Part Two focuses on the speech itself.

The following areas are covered in detail:

Part One

- ❋ The appointment of the best man: let the groom know he's chosen the right man.

- ❋ Dealing diplomatically with the in-laws: this sometimes calls for supreme tact.

- ❋ The engagement party: your first chance to meet everyone involved in the wedding.

- ❋ Organizing and executing a brilliant stag party: how to do it with military precision and ensure everyone has a great time.

- ❋ A step-by-step guide to the best man's duties in the run-up to the wedding: there's a lot more to remember than just the ring.

- ❋ The wedding rehearsal: your last chance to smooth out any potential problems.

- ❋ The actual ceremony: how to look after the groom, organize the ushers and direct the guests.

- ❋ The reception: there could be anything from 20 to 200 guests and you're expected to help look after them.

- ❋ The end of the party: oversee the departure of the guests and help the happy couple get away on their honeymoon.

Part Two

- ❋ The speech: how to write, practise and deliver a funny and unforgettable speech.

The advice given in this book will help you no matter what type of wedding you are taking part in, since many of the best man's duties are the same whatever the scale, venue or religion. Just pick out the parts that are relevant to the type of wedding that you are going to be involved in. In Chapter 7 (see pages 67–73) I have detailed some of the wedding customs of different cultures and religions.

Origins of the role

There are several theories as to how the role of best man first came about. Some believe the role traces its origins back to the time of the Germanic Goths during the latter days of the Roman Empire. Back then it was usual for a man to marry within his own community. Often there weren't enough women to go around, in which case nuptially inclined young men were forced to look elsewhere for a bride. This situation called for visits to women in neighbouring villages. Hardly surprisingly, these unsuspecting women (not to mention their irate fathers) didn't look too kindly upon being kidnapped by a hairy Goth. Along with their families they often put up quite a fight. It was the best man's job to physically support the potential groom during the kidnap process and later at the ceremony, when the bride's father and brothers would often turn up to wrestle the girl back.

Nowadays we'd hope that most brides, and most fathers of the bride for that matter, would have given their consent to the marriage. Therefore the best man's support is more moral and emotional than physical. But during the ceremony he still stands on the right of his groom and the bride, ready to defend them, should the need arise.

This book won't instruct you how to fight off the bride's irate family (I'll leave you to figure that one out for yourself should the unfortunate situation arise), but what it will do is help you to be the best best man you can possibly be.

BEST MAN'S DUTIES

'He is the best man who, when making his plans,
fears and reflects on everything that can happen
to him, but in the moment of action is bold.'

Herodotus
Greek historian

Chapter One

The Appointment

It rarely comes completely out of the blue. Unless you're old friends who haven't seen one another in years, or you live across the other side of the world, it's likely you will see the occasion of your appointment coming. It normally happens like this: a couple of weeks after your friend has announced that he and his girlfriend are getting engaged you get a low-key invitation to meet him at the pub. 'Nothing special,' he says, 'just you and me for a quiet drink.' The instant you realize that the rest of the lads won't be coming too, you should smell a rat. This isn't going to be any ordinary drink. You need to go along prepared for this one. It's going to be the big question.

The appointment of the best man can be a scary task – both for the intended best man and for the future groom. I've heard of grooms getting themselves into a terrible state over the whole situation. How should I go about doing it? What if my best man doesn't want to be my best man? What if he doesn't approve of my wife? Some fiancés approach the best man proposal with almost as much dread as the actual marriage proposal. This is just silly. There's no need to make a song and a dance out of it. It's highly likely that you, the future best man, know you're going to be asked. And it's also highly likely that the future groom knows that you know you're going to be asked. Just make sure you make things as comfortable as you can for your groom when he asks you and put him at ease. It's not like he has to get down on one knee with a ring and a bunch of roses! Just buying you a few drinks should suffice.

Oh, and don't hesitate too long before you accept the job. In all but the very rarest of situations you should have seen the request coming and you should already have made up your mind. If you ask for a few days to think about it then the groom will never be entirely sure that you are truly committed to your role. One short-lived best man I once knew took over a week to get back to his friend after he was originally asked. By the time he gave his answer, which incidentally was 'Yes', the groom had already appointed someone else. They were never quite the same close friends ever again.

Be committed

So let's presume you have accepted your role. Let's face it, if you'd turned him down you'd hardly be reading this book, would you? The first thing you should do is convince the groom that you are 100 percent committed to being the best best man possible. Tell him what a great woman he is marrying and remind him that you are available to help both of them with the wedding preparations in any way you can.

You should arrange to meet with the couple as soon as possible to get an idea of the kind of wedding it is going to be and to discuss exactly what duties they want you to undertake. This is a good chance to show the bride-to-be what a superb organizer you are, how responsible you can be, how cool you are under pressure and how willing you are to help. Getting married is an extremely stressful period in any couple's life. Don't forget that you are there to help things go smoothly – both on the wedding day and in the months leading up to it.

I know of one best man who was faced with a very tricky situation indeed. His soon-to-be-married friends were finding that their wedding plans were spiralling completely out of control and causing a lot of unnecessary tension between them. At this stressful time, even the smallest things can cause a disagreement. The best man found himself having to step in at various hairy moments to calm things down when the couple started arguing about caterers, florists, parents-in-law, pageboys, table plans, the colour of the napkins, etc, etc. Without taking sides, 'bestie' managed to settle virtually every dispute they had. (The napkin colour dilemma, however, was never properly resolved and, to this day, the groom still cannot tell the difference between burnt orange and fuchsia.) Other friends now reckon their best man may have saved their marriage before it had even started. Fortunately bride and groom are still happily married. They are forever grateful to him for his delicate mediation skills.

Meet the parents

As the best man you should make contact with both the bride's and groom's parents early on in the engagement. You'll meet the parents at the engagement party of course, but it's a good idea to visit them, or at least speak to them on the phone, beforehand. The more people that are reassured of how competent and responsible you are, the smoother the whole wedding build-up and day will be. Even if you already know one or both sets of parents, talk to the bride and groom before making contact. You should tread carefully if the parents are separated or there are step-parents involved; again check with the bride and groom as to who you should be making contact with.

Qualities a best man needs

Marriage status

Tradition used to demand that the best man should be a bachelor.
That way, if the groom was (due to various unforseen circumstances,
like a change of mind or death) unable to fulfil his duty and marry
his bride, then the best man could step in and fill his shoes.
Nowadays, you'll be happy to know, you are no longer required
to act as replacement groom and no one will expect you to be
unmarried. In fact, if you've already been through the marriage
experience yourself, you're likely to make a better go of it as
best man. You'll know exactly what the groom's up against.

Sobriety

No one wants to hear a slurred best man's speech. It may be
funny for the first couple of minutes, but after a while the guests
will lose their patience.

You've also got to maintain a certain level-headedness during
the stag celebrations. Of course you're not expected to remain
completely sober, but it is up to you to get the groom back home
in one piece. This means you'll have to be sober enough to at least
dial the number of a taxi firm on your mobile phone.

Punctuality

Some grooms are so nervous that they lose the ability to tell the
time, let alone remember to put on their watch the morning of
the big day. Timekeeping is very much your job. If the groom is
late you'll get the blame. If the ushers are late you'll get the blame.
If you're late, no one will speak to you for the rest of the day.

Responsibility

There's no doubting that it's stressful being a best man. With so
many things to remember and organize, there are going to be times
when you wonder why you agreed to take on the job. But with lots

of preparation and clear thinking you'll make the groom and his wife a very happy couple and you'll have a great day yourself. If you're methodical you can make sure there are no mishaps.

Tact

After the bride and groom, you are the person next in line in the spotlight. Like it or not, people will be watching you. You will already know a lot of the guests, and no one's expecting you to put on airs, but there are certain times when you will need to be very tactful. For example, it's your job to get everyone from the marriage venue to the reception. When you deliver your speech you need to remember that your audience ranges from 5-year-old bridesmaids to 95-year-old grannies. A certain diplomacy will be expected. Don't be prudish, but do be prudent.

Presentability

A friend of mine insisted on choosing his best friend as his best man. Nothing unusual about that you might think. Except when I tell you that his best friend was scruffy, drunken and unhygienic. We all warned the groom, but he wouldn't have any of it. He dug his heels in and appointed his unkempt friend as best man. It was a case of the groom and the ungroomed.

Sure enough, the big day came and there was the best man with a shabby suit, old, unpolished shoes, loosened tie, straggly, greasy hair, and a cigarette permanently lodged in the side of his mouth. Fortunately the tails of his morning suit hid the fact that his shirt wasn't even tucked in.

If your usual style could be described as scruffy, shabby or indeed any other word that means the same thing, you're going to have to accept that you'll have to undergo a bit of a makeover.

Communication skills

Communicating with people is one of your key jobs on the day – sorting out the ushers, making sure that the guests are okay, directing people to the reception venue and, of course, the speech. Although other people will make speeches at the wedding, it is the best man's speech that is the most anticipated. This doesn't, however, mean that you have to be a stand-up comedian or a latter-day Martin Luther King. No one is expecting a professional level address. They want to laugh, yes. They perhaps want to be moved somewhat. But they all know you are a normal bloke who happens to be very good friends with the groom.

If you feel your communication skills could use a little work, then you can always practise them to build up your confidence. More on that later (see page 109).

Chapter Two

Engagement Party

Not every couple will have an engagement party. If they don't, then in some ways you can count yourself lucky – that's one less best man duty on your list of things to do. But if they do, then it's crucial that you attend. After the bride, groom and their immediate family members, you and the maid of honour are the next most important guests. Turn up and make sure you're on time.

View the engagement party as your first chance to gauge how things might pan out on the big day. It's by no means a rehearsal (most engagement parties are simply a chance for all the friends and family to meet and share a few drinks) but it will give you an invaluable insight into potential pitfalls and problem family members. It will also give you the chance to meet many of the other wedding guests.

This is the evening when you first meet the bride's antisocial brother. It is also your chance to witness Auntie Dot's gin-drinking abilities first hand. Above all, it is an opportunity for you to really shine and reassure both sets of parents that you are without doubt the best man for the job. Make an effort to circulate and find out who's who. It will make things easier on the wedding day when you have to inform Sally and Mark that their three-year-old son is systematically dismantling the wedding cake.

I heard of a very posh engagement party a couple of years ago when the bride's and groom's parents met for the first time. It was on neutral territory and everyone expected proceedings to run as smoothly as the copious supply of alcohol. That was the problem. There was too much alcohol. The bride's mother had about three bottles of champagne to herself and made what she thought was a fairly innocuous comment about the groom's mother's party dress. The latter took offence and uttered similar comments about the former's hairdo. Needless to say, maternal relations remained frosty until well after the wedding day.

However, because the best man was aware of this initial personality clash it meant that he was able to keep both mothers apart on the wedding day and thereby avoid unnecessary confrontation. If the best man belongs to neither family he is in a prime position to act as go-between and peace negotiator – a delicate task indeed.

Incidentally, the way you present yourself during the engagement party is crucial. If you turn up late in scruffy clothes and proceed to drink the bar dry then everyone concerned will spend the run-up to the wedding worrying that you'll do the same on the big day. Reassure the bride, groom and both families by playing it cool.

Chapter Three

Stag Party

What used to be a single evening spent in a pub followed by some very inept dancing in a nightclub, has now turned into a major social event, often lasting over a long weekend. There may be three evenings to coordinate, two activity days to arrange, flights abroad that need to be booked and 20 rowdy stags who need marshalling. Some stags even have two stag dos – perhaps a small evening party for work colleagues and then a weekend for close friends. Whatever your plans turn out to be, believe me, the whole event needs to be organized with military precision, otherwise it will soon descend into chaos.

The stag do is what separates best men from worst men. It is where you will stand or fall. Aside from the wedding speech, it is the duty that you will be most remembered for and most judged on. Make sure you get it right and plan early.

Choosing the stags

One thing you can guarantee about all of the groom's closest friends is that they will not necessarily get on with each other as well as they get on with the groom. How on earth can you expect Ian the IT expert to have anything in common with Mad Dog Mitchell? When coming up with a list of stags, there's no point simply asking the groom for a list of his top 15 friends. There are some far more tricky aspects to consider.

Will they make an effort to get on with the other stags?

The last thing you want on the stag do is for the group to split into several small cliques. I have a friend who was brought up in France and who finished his schooling in Britain. Rather foolishly he invited both his French and British friends on his stag do. Through no fault of their own, other than an inability to comprehend one another, the group immediately split into two and the groom was left trying to bridge the gap. He spent more of the weekend translating jokes that were barely funny in the first place than he did enjoying himself. It would have been far better if he'd thrown two stag parties – one for the Frogs and one for the Rosbifs.

Can they afford it?

With stag weekends regularly costing up to £1,000 per person nowadays, especially if foreign flights and hotels are involved, there's nothing more embarrassing than arriving at your destination only to find that a couple of guys have already run out of money. On my own stag weekend, one of my best friends was unemployed at the time and couldn't afford to stay in our hotel with us. He ended up sleeping in the back of his car, which broke up the group somewhat. He also looked and smelled like he'd slept in a ditch. In fact, come to think of it, maybe he did sleep in a ditch!

Does the groom know this guy well enough to go out on his own for a drink with him?

There's no point inviting transient friends along. A stag do is a chance for the groom to officially acknowledge someone as a close friend. A bloke he hit it off with down the pub last week does not count.

Will he add to the groom's enjoyment of the stag do?

Your groom really won't want to spend time wishing he hadn't invited a certain person along. This is well worth remembering if he plans to invite old friends he hasn't seen or been in contact with for ages. I heard about one groom who asked along an old friend from primary school who had since emigrated to Australia. It seems the friend had spent the intervening years decorating himself with rather unsavoury tattoos and cultivating a serious drinking habit. Fortunately for the rest of the stags he spent most of the weekend curled up in a drunken heap on the floor of his hotel room.

In times past it was traditional to invite both the groom's and the bride's father along on the stag do. No one will expect you to do that nowadays. Okay, so it might work if you're marrying one of Ozzy Osbourne's daughters — in fact it would probably liven up proceedings — but most of the stags would think it odd if there was a paternal element to the party. Especially if that paternal element was the one giving away the bride. Whatever they said, other stags would feel distinctly uncomfortable sharing a rowdy evening with the groom's father or future father-in-law. What if a visit to a strip club was part of the evening's entertainment?

Having said this, it is of course a matter of personal choice for the groom. He and his friends may get on so well with his father that it would be odd not to invite him along. Indeed his Dad might be an Ozzy Osbourne wannabe, but do think about what effect his presence will have on the party.

It's a good idea to invite along any brother of the bride. The groom may not yet be friends with his future brother-in-law, in which case the latter will probably make his excuses. But it would certainly be very politic to give him the choice.

Choosing the right stags is a complicated business. It's well worth setting aside a whole evening to sit down with the groom and finalize the invitation list. Think of the stag do as a cooking recipe. If you don't get the correct ingredients (the right stags) then you haven't got a chance of creating a tasty dish that everyone will enjoy.

Deciding what do do

It doesn't even have to be a boozy, raucous affair if this isn't the groom's style and there's nothing wrong with simply making an evening of it in your local town, having a meal and a few drinks. But most grooms want something a bit more adventurous these days. If everyone can afford it, why not spend a long weekend somewhere? Why not go abroad for a couple of days to Barcelona, Prague, Amsterdam or Dublin? Or if you're feeling really flush, maybe New York or Las Vegas?

The revolution in air travel, particularly short-haul flights, makes it much cheaper and easier to fly to a foreign destination. Travel companies have realized how much potential there is in both the stag- and the hen-weekend market. If you let a professional stag organization company help you out it may cost a bit more, but it will cut down your list of best man duties.

Spending a weekend away is a great leveller and the perfect way to get all the stags bonding. If no one has been to the destination before and, even better, if you're abroad and no one speaks the local lingo, then you'll find that everyone rallies together in the face of a common enemy, so to speak. People are also far more likely to let their hair down and act like fools when they're in a foreign country – which is a successful ingredient to any stag weekend.

I have a friend who is a lawyer and one of the most cautious, law-abiding men I know. Partly because of his profession he never steps out of line and wouldn't dream of misbehaving in public. Yet the two times I've been abroad on stag weekends with him I've finally seen his true colours emerge.

Away from home he knew his job was not at risk if he was to overindulge on the booze and have a minor brush with the law. In fact, despite a severe lack of sobriety, he actually managed to remain in control. But simply the knowledge that he could really let loose if he wanted to meant he had a far more enjoyable time than normal. Consequently, so did everyone else.

Ultimately it's the groom's decision as to where you all go and what you do. He will, however, appreciate guidance from you. Don't pressurize him into doing anything or going anywhere he'd prefer not to. Although you're organizing the do, this is his celebration and your main concern is that he has a great time. Bear in mind what kind of person he is and what type of stags he's inviting along. Sky-diving, strip clubs and rivers of booze are not everyone's cup of tea. On the following pages you'll find a few suggestions for fun activities for a stag do.

Activity days

Rally driving, paintballing, parachuting, hunting, flying lesson, gliding, abseiling, bungee jumping, kayaking, surfing, deep-sea fishing, hang-gliding, go-karting, greyhound racing, horse racing, paragliding, quad bikes, tank driving, water skiing, power boating – and that's just for starters. There are so many activities on offer that are suitable for a stag activity day. If you've got money to burn you can even drive a Formula One car around a racetrack or co-pilot a Russian MIG in the skies above Moscow.

Find out from the groom what kind of activities he'd like to do. And use your email circulars (see page 33) to ascertain how much the other stags are willing to pay. It may end up that you all just go for a round of golf. But the advantage of more extreme activities is that they very quickly break the ice if the stags don't all know one another and, more importantly, they offer tempting chances to play practical jokes and ridicule the groom. Just make sure he doesn't break any bones.

I will never forget the story of the army officer whose best man arranged for him and his army friends to spend a stag weekend in Snowdonia. As you can expect with a group of off-duty soldiers, the mood was fairly boisterous. In his infinite wisdom, 'bestie' had arranged for all the boys to go quad biking over some pretty dangerous Welsh terrain. Stupidly, someone thought it would be a good idea to bring along a crate of beers, most of it destined for the throat of the groom.

You can guess what happened. The groom got drunk, lost control of his quad bike and ended up breaking his left arm. His fellow stags thought it was hilarious, but when the best man had to explain to the bride-to-be what had happened, she almost broke his left arm too.

On activity days it's essential to stay off the booze until the dangerous part is over. If you're simply playing golf then you can all drink as much as you like (well, within reason unless you want to get thrown off the course). But if the day's action involves motorized vehicles and a certain manual dexterity and a risk of bodily damage, then you're going to need to remain in charge of your faculties. Booze and tank driving or flying lessons simply do not mix. Most stag activity organizers are well trained in spotting, and smelling, anyone who's been drinking.

There are loads of companies out there who will organize a stag activity for you (see pages 122–4). A quick search on the internet will pull up dozens of businesses vying for your custom. Simply type your chosen activity and the word 'stag' into a search engine and see what comes up. Give the company a call and find out a little more about what they do before booking anything. Make sure that the company or operator you use is fully insured against accident and injury.

It sounds obvious, but the best activities for group bonding are the ones where you remain in a group. Driving Formula One cars may sound like a great laugh, but it's a solitary activity, as is gliding or flying. On the other hand, spending the day paintballing may be a bit unadventurous, but at least you're all in a team together. Ultimately it's the company and sharing the experience that's more important than the adrenalin.

Sporting events

Getting a large number of tickets for a Premiership football match is about as easy as figuring out why England haven't won the World Cup since 1966. Nevertheless if you book through an agency or you opt for a less popular sport instead you may have more luck. A Saturday afternoon sporting event can be a great way to get the party going, especially if you all have some money riding on the outcome. What about a day at the races?

Golf

Golf is now the number one participation sport on stag dos, partly because it's so sociable and partly because it's easy to handicap everyone and even things out. The only problem is that you'll have to split up a large group of stags – it's impractical to send out groups of more than four players.

As a rule, it's best not to tell the golf club that you are all on a stag do. They'll only worry about drinking on the course and rowdy behaviour. Just tell them it's a business trip and keep your voices down until you're all past the third hole.

You may well have a few non-golfers among your group, but because golf is such an adaptable sport this shouldn't pose too many problems. Here are a few ways to ensure that whatever the skill levels, everyone should get a good hit.

Best ball – Split the stags into teams. The idea is to make sure each team finishes the round with the lowest score. After each team member has made his first drive the team keeps the best drive and picks up the other balls. The team then all play their second balls from the spot where the best first drive landed. Again they keep the best shot and pick up the other balls before playing them from the position of the best second shot. This continues all the way to the green and until the first player reaches the hole.

Three club – Each player chooses three clubs and is limited to using only these clubs throughout the whole round. You then have to hit your shots using your clubs in strict sequence – no matter what shot you are going for. Laugh at each other as you inevitably end up driving with a putter on certain holes or putting with a driver. This is a great way to equalize different skill levels and is quite a laugh too, as you can imagine. Some people insist that everyone have the same three clubs: a driver, a sand wedge and a putter. Just don't let the groundsmen spot you.

Speed golf – Each player carries just one club with him and has to run around the course in between shots. Don't worry, no one is allowed to play the ball as if it's a hockey match, since points are awarded for both speed and the number of shots required to complete the course. So even though you run, you do have to stop and play each shot properly.

Evening entertainment

This can be more difficult to organize than the daytime activity. If you're intending to have a boozy evening, the presence of vast amounts of alcohol means individual egos soon start to take over. What you don't want is different stags arguing over what the course of action should be. Decide on a plan well beforehand and stick to it. Otherwise the group will split up and the evening will rapidly deteriorate. Remember, you're in charge.

If you're all on a stag weekend then meet up in the hotel bar. Start off with a top-notch meal. Again, if it's going to be a raucous evening rather than a sedate meal with a small glass of port and a cigar, think about asking the hotel or restaurant whether they have a private dining room. These are designed with stag parties in mind since they allow you get away with the type of boozing and boisterous behaviour that wouldn't be tolerated in the main restaurant. Anyone who's seen a group of stags in a restaurant will know full well that no one wants to witness their shenanigans. Nor will many of the stags want their shenanigans witnessed by normal law-abiding people. The table manners alone will be enough to put off other more civilized eaters.

After dinner what you don't want to do is simply head off to a drinking establishment. Ideally you need some sort of focus to the evening. Something like a pool tournament or ten pin bowling may not be tremendously exciting, but what about a night of greyhound

Being the best woman at a stag party

Hey, it's the 21st century. Having a best woman occurs more often nowadays than you'd think. And if a groom's best friend is female, or his sister, why shouldn't he choose her as his best (wo)man?

If you are the best woman, there are certain practicalities to consider: your idea of a stag do is likely to be a little different. It's also unlikely that you'll be keen on visiting a strip club. But don't be bothered about this. If the groom expected to be entertained by naked ladies then he wouldn't have asked you to be his best woman. Just think about the plus points of your stag do – it's highly likely that it will be better organized, since women are almost always better than men at arranging social events. The other big plus is that as you're new to all this you may well come up with something a lot more original.

A couple of years ago a female friend of my mother's was appointed best woman to her best friend. Her job involved the initially rather unenviable task of marshalling 12 rowdy men through the stag evening. Many of them were sceptical that she, as a woman, was up to the job. Instead of opting for the obvious bar, restaurant, bar, nightclub combination, she booked everyone into a luxurious spa hotel for the afternoon. For most of the men present it was their first experience of being massaged, pampered, manicured, pedicured and generally beautified. After they had overcome their initial macho cynicism they all began to unwind, had a wonderful time and left relaxed and rejuvenated. Out of respect for tradition, the female bestie then took them all down the pub afterwards.

racing, a rock concert or a trip to the local casino? Oh, and don't make the mistake that a close friend of mine did. As best man he was of course in charge of the kitty (see page 34). The minute he was let loose in the casino he stuck all the money on the roulette table. Of course he lost the lot. He also lost the respect of the groom and all his fellow stags.

Many nightclubs and casinos are distinctly stag-unfriendly. Hardly surprising – the last thing they want is a 15-strong rabble of boozy lads invading their premises. There are two ways to get round this problem. Either call a few days in advance to put your names on the door, or else split the group up into threes and fours and stagger

Stag night practical jokes

First of all it's traditional to make the groom wear utterly embarrassing clothing for the crucial stages of the stag do. A simple way to do this is to buy some tasteless clothing in a charity shop the day before the stag weekend starts. Force the groom to wear these clothes during the daytime or evening entertainment. (See page 124 for party supplies.)

Comedy breasts are always a big favourite, as is an old floral pattern dress and women's underwear. The character and spirit of your groom will determine just how outrageous a costume you can make him wear. It takes a real man to wear drag on his stag do and his friends will respect him forever if he does.

On my own stag weekend I was forced to wear a tight, sleeveless belly-button T-shirt with the word 'Princess' emblazoned across the front, a pair of pink baggy trousers and a little purple clip-on bow tie. Then, to my embarrassment, I learned we were to spend the evening at a greyhound track. The shaven-haired, tattooed men at the racetrack bar raised a few eyebrows, but fortunately I got through the evening relatively unscathed.

If the groom does agree to wear women's clothing and carry an inflatable sheep around all night (under peer pressure – it's not like he'll have a choice) he will feel a lot better if everyone else makes a bit of an effort too. Why not get T-shirts printed up for all the rest of the stags to wear? (See page 124 for companies that offer this service.) This way the groom will look more like the butt of a practical joke and less like a deranged person who got dressed in the dark.

Don't forget, however, that if an upmarket bar or nightclub is part of the evening's entertainment, then you will need smart clothes to change into later. However much you charm the bouncer, he will not let a man wearing a dress and comedy breasts pass through his doors.

Any groom worth his salt will expect some sort of practical joke. Strippers dressed as policewomen; shaved eyebrows; groom handcuffed half naked to a lamp post; groom abandoned with no phone and no money... the list of ideas is long and there are always laughs to be had at the groom's expense. Just don't take the joke too far – as the best man you know the groom well and should judge what he will and won't find amusing. Also consider what the bride's reaction will be. The basic rules are: don't do anything that is going to affect his appearance for the wedding or anything potentially terrifying, injurious or dangerous. In particular, don't do anything that could get you locked up in jail, especially in a foreign country. You may be stuck there for weeks. Practical jokes are supposed to add to the enjoyment of the evening, not frighten the groom to death and spoil the wedding photos.

I heard of one stag weekend recently in Estonia, in eastern Europe. The stag party had just arrived at the activity centre where they'd booked a day of military games when suddenly a van screeched to a halt in front of them. Out of the back of the van jumped five huge thugs armed with rifles and wearing balaclavas. They promptly grabbed the groom, manhandled him into the back of the van and drove off into the woods.

It turned out that the best man had arranged the kidnapping as part of an elaborate practical trick. The poor groom had no idea and assumed he was about to come to an awful end, miles from home, courtesy of a bullet from a gangster's Kalashnikov. Unfortunately for all concerned he decided his only course of action was to fight his way out of the back of the van. He managed to inflict some serious punches on the actors he believed were Mafia thugs, but when he heroically jumped from the moving van he broke his collarbone.

He laughed about it all afterwards – several months afterwards.

Cameras or no cameras?

The groom does not want to worry about pictures of him appearing on a website the day before he gets married. He certainly doesn't want his bride or her family to see evidence of his stag-do exploits.

You can't, of course, ban cameras from the stag weekend. In fact you'll want to record some of the funnier incidents during the daytime activities. But, as best man, you should ensure that no photographic devices are anywhere to be seen once the sun's gone down. In any case, blow-up dolls and inflatable sheep never look their best under flash exposure.

your entry. On my stag weekend my best man had to phone the nightclubs a couple of weeks beforehand and supply the names, addresses and occupations of every member of our party. We still managed to get thrown out of one of them.

Many stag nights end up with some sort of underdressed female entertainment. It's not every groom's idea of fun – and for goodness sake don't let his bride-to-be find out – but it's the one time in his life when he can look at other naked ladies without feeling guilty or sleazy. It's a centuries-old tradition dating back to ancient Greek times, so it would be churlish not to see some female flesh. But it is of course a personal choice for the groom. Don't pressurize him. If he wants to abstain, for the sake of his conscience and his wife-to-be, then let him and respect him for it.

Organizing the stag celebrations

Once you've helped the groom to choose his trusty wingmen and decided where you're going to go and what you're going to do, it's now up to you to start organizing things. Believe me, you can't start early enough on this task.

Traditionally, stag celebrations used to be held on the Thursday or Friday before a Saturday wedding. Don't even think about doing it this close to the wedding. You need as much time as possible for the bruises to heal, the hangover to wear off and the eyebrow hair to grow back. Instead hold it a couple of weekends before the big day. In any case, the evening before the wedding will probably be taken up with a family dinner (see page 47).

Start off by phoning all the chosen stags and extending an official invitation. Make a note of each one's email address and send all of them, including the groom, two or three provisional dates for the big celebration. You can guarantee that not everyone will be able to make the same evening or weekend, but if you offer a few dates then you'll probably be able to accommodate most of the people on the list. There are always a couple of the groom's friends who can't make it. You'll just have to decide with the groom whether, as guests, they are so important that you need to reschedule the whole thing. Sometimes on a weekend stag celebration you'll find that certain stags can make part of the weekend but not all of it. This is not ideal, but it's better than not having them come at all. It simply involves more organizing for you.

Keeping track of everyone who has been invited is very complicated. Make a list of who's committed to coming and whether they have covered any payment or deposits that you may need from them. On a stag weekend there will be lots of hotels, restaurants and events to book. Be meticulous and keep a written record of who has paid for what (see The financial side, below).

Set up two circular email lists to all the stags – one that includes the groom and one that doesn't. This way you can keep the groom abreast of all the timings and travel arrangements, but keep him in the dark when it comes to what activities and entertainment are involved and how you plan to stitch him up. Yes, well and truly stitch him up you must (see Stag night practical jokes pages 30–1). This is all part and parcel of the stag celebrations. No proper stag do is complete without it.

Keep communicating with the stags

Send regular emails updating the stags on what's planned, when it's happening and where you'll all be going. Email banter can be a great way for stags initially to get to know one another. It will also get everyone in the mood for the stag celebrations.

Get hold of mobile phone numbers for everyone coming on the stag do. Plug all these numbers into your own phone. On a stag weekend, especially if you're moving around, it's easy to lose the odd person. You need to keep the troops together at all times.

You're not required to be everyone's babysitter, but if foreign travel is involved then check that everyone has set up their phones to function abroad. It may also be an idea to remind them all to check they have travel insurance and visas where necessary.

The financial side

Get a firm commitment on numbers from everyone invited as soon as possible. You may be required to put down a deposit on hotel accommodation and pay for flights well in advance. Unless you have a particularly generous bank manager, you'll need to get cheques from everyone to cover this. The financial side of the stag do can be the most stressful part. I would advise you not to book anything until you have received money from all, or virtually all of the stags. It is always the best man who ends up paying for any shortfall. And you can't exactly ask the groom to pay for financially errant friends.

In fact, with the possible exception of foreign flights, the groom traditionally shouldn't pay for anything. No one will mind if you spread out all of his costs among you and the rest of the stags. Between 10 or 15 of you this won't work out to be a huge amount. The groom will probably be spending huge amounts of his own money on his wedding and will appreciate the gesture.

One area that can be tricky to organize is the buying of drinks. Let's face it: on most stag dos there is going to be drinking. If the rounds of drinks aren't seen to be fair, some of the stags are going to get upset. The way to deal with this is to use the whip-round system. At the beginning of the evening or weekend ask all the stags (except for the groom, of course) to hand over enough money for say 10 drinks. Collect that money together, add your own contribution and place it all in one wallet that you'll then keep in a safe pocket. From then on the wallet will be known as 'the kitty' and all drinks should be bought using money from it.

Since there may be 10 or 15 stags, inevitably different people will drink at different speeds. While Mad Dog Mitchell, for example, can down three pints in 20 minutes, Ian the IT expert may well take a whole hour to get through a small glass of white wine. This, I am afraid, is all part and parcel of a lively stag do. It's tough luck, really, for the slow drinkers. What you cannot be expected to do, as best man, is to monitor who's drinking what and who owes how much to the kitty. Everyone has to simply enter into the spirit of things and donate the same amount, regardless of how much they plan to consume. If you think this may cause problems then you should warn people before the start of the stag do.

I remember being at one stag evening in a very expensive drinking club. The majority of the stags rather wisely stuck to beer for most of the evening, but a couple of jokers thought they'd spend all night downing champagne, expensive cocktails and fine brandies. It was funny at first, but since we were all in a whip-round, some people soon got a little annoyed. What you don't want is resentment on a stag do because someone isn't pulling his weight financially. In fact, what normally happens is that the kitty soon runs out and those that are drinking less go to bed before the hard-core contingent. Late drinkers then do a second whip-round and start up another kitty. But of course you don't want the group splitting off early into different cliques and buying rounds separately. The whole idea of a stag do is for the groom's best friends to bond together before he gets married. This means drinking together, too.

Meeting up

If the stag do is just an evening out then this is easy. Meet in a centrally located pub and start the night from there. But where should you meet up if you're all embarking on a stag weekend? One great way to get the party going is to hire a limousine to transport you all to the stag venue (see page 124). Meet in a pub and arrange for the limo driver to pick you all up after work on a Friday. Then bundle everyone into the limo, champagne and all. By the time you reach your destination you'll all have a few drinks inside you and everyone in the group will know one another. Once you've split the cost of the limo between all of you it might actually work out cheaper than taking the train or a hiring a fleet of taxis.

For domestic stag weekends the train station is of course the other option. Nearly every large railway terminus has a pub or bar. They're hardly the most refined of establishments – at the beginning of my stag weekend we had trouble persuading the station tramp that he wasn't invited – but they are the perfect meeting point. There is no chance on Earth that all the stags will arrive on time. As they turn up at staggered intervals, you'll be glad that you have a base where everyone can meet. This is the opportunity for any stags who don't already know one another to break the ice.

For stag weekends abroad, airport pubs and bars are the best places to meet. It's worth considering paying that little bit extra and booking everyone into the business or first-class lounge.

You don't have to be flying luxury to avail yourselves of such places. Just phone ahead and book the group in. But a word of caution. Don't tell them you're on a stag trip. Say it's a business or golfing trip instead. And take it easy on the sauce. Airline operators won't let you on the plane nowadays if they suspect you're drunk. It's just not worth the security risk.

Don't overdo the booze

No one is expecting you to stay sober – that would be patently ridiculous. Besides, you'll be expected to get things going on the drinks front and encourage a party atmosphere from the very start. However, you don't want to get blind drunk. If anyone's, that's the job of the groom. Remember that you're in charge of the evening, from start to finish. You've got to get everyone together at the beginning and you've got to get the groom home at the end of the evening. He may have drunk so much that he can barely remember his own name, let alone where he's staying that night. It's your job to get him tucked up safely in bed in one piece.

Oh, and if your stag evening is taking place in the same town that his fiancée lives in, or if they already share a home, whatever you do, don't let him get ideas about going home to her after a boozy evening. Can you imagine her face when he turns up at her door at 3 a.m., dishevelled and stinking of booze. In fact, don't even let him call her. His slurred speech will only make her worry he's done something he shouldn't have.

An old friend of mine had his stag night in London and never even considered that it might be a good idea to stay somewhere other than at his (and his fiancée's) flat. Before the wedding I witnessed her berating the best man for letting his protegé get in the state he did. Apparently she had been woken up at 4 a.m. by her husband-to-be banging on their front door. When she opened it he staggered in dressed in nothing but his underpants and a ripped, lipstick-stained shirt. His breath smelt like a distillery. To avoid incurring the wrath of the fiancée, the best man had deposited the drunken groom outside his flat and driven off in a taxi. Needless to say, the fiancée's wrath had lasted for a good few days.

Chapter Four

Countdown to the Big Day

The countdown to the wedding is a bit like a NASA countdown to the launch of one of its rockets. The schedule takes eons of planning and starts to get more and more demanding the nearer you get to take-off. The weeks before the wedding are always fraught with stress for both the bride and the groom. No wedding would be complete without these last minute hiccups. Your job is to help iron out as many of the problems as possible, be on hand whenever you can to help and act as a sympathetic ear when it all simply gets too much.

The best man: a pre-wedding checklist

12 months to go

- You are appointed as best man.
- Make a note in your diary of wedding date and keep the week before wedding clear as your services will be needed!

9 months to go

- Engagement party.

5 months to go

- Help groom to choose the ushers.
- Start organizing the stag party or weekend away.

4 months to go

- Discuss wedding plans with the bride and groom so that you know who other members of wedding party are.
- Make sure you know what the transport arrangements are.
- Go with groom to choose wedding outfits.

3 months to go

- Start writing your speech.
- Buy gift and card for the wedding couple.

2 months to go

- Regularly practise your speech.
- Confirm all of the arrangements for the stag party/weekend.

4 weeks to go

- The stag party/weekend.

3 weeks to go

- Prepare and send duty list for the ushers; call them to confirm what they are doing, what time they need to arrive, etc.
- Visit wedding and reception venue with the bride and groom to familiarize yourself with route, parking arrangements, etc.
- Confirm order of speeches with bride and groom.
- Check the groom has the wedding ring.

2 weeks to go

- Finalize speech.

1 week to go

- Attend wedding rehearsal and dinner.
- Collect order of ceremony sheets.
- Go with groom to collect hired clothing.
- Confirm arrangements for collecting buttonholes from bride.
- Check with groom that all honeymoon arrangements have been confirmed.
- Buy or collect decorations for couple's getaway car.
- Give the bride and groom their gift and card from you.

1 day to go

- Charge up your mobile phone.
- Withdraw plenty of cash.
- Collect letters and cards from absent friends from bride's (and possibly groom's) family.
- Check that the groom has the ring, knows where it is and that it is somewhere safe.

Help the groom

Your main role in the run-up to the wedding is to support the groom and offer whatever help he needs. Stay in touch on a regular basis – this will not only help him, but it will help you be a better best man as you'll be fully aware of the arrangements. The week leading up to the big day is when your duties as right-hand man really come into their own. The groom will be nervous and forgetful. It's your job to calm his nerves and remind him of the things he has to do.

Transport

It's not your job to arrange the transport for the wedding day, this is down to the groom, but you are responsible on the day for making sure that everyone gets to where they need to be and on time, so you need to be aware of the transport arrangements that have been made. Make sure that you know how everyone is travelling and who with. Make a note of the contact numbers for the companies or individuals involved and jot down the telephone numbers of a couple of local taxi firms just in case anything goes wrong and you need an alternative way to transport people.

Clothing

This of course all depends on the formality and style of the wedding. The groom and his wife-to-be will have the ultimate say in this and, as best man, you should, quite literally, follow suit. I've been to some weddings where if the best man had worn a morning suit he would have looked quite ridiculous compared to everyone else. Equally I've been to some weddings where any guest not in a morning suit would have been very much frowned upon.

More and more grooms are choosing to dress themselves, their best man and all the ushers in matching suits. Whether the husband-to-be opts for lounge suits, black tie or morning dress, if it's smart looks, style and panache he's after then he can't do better than kit out all his closest friends in matching suits and ties. However, hiring five or six identical suits can be costly and it is usually the bride and groom who bear this cost. Some couples may be happy for the male members of the wedding

How to tie a cravat

Drape the cravat around your neck with the short end hanging to the left side of your chest.

Take the long end in your right hand and cross it over the short end.

Tuck the long end underneath the short end so it's now hanging on the right-hand side of your chest.

Wrap the long end over the short end again so it's hanging to the left-hand side of your chest.

Bring the long end up through the loop that you have now created.

If you want to wear a self-tie cravat then just hang the long end down the front of your chest, tighten the knot and secure it all with a cravat pin.

For a scrunchy tie, ignore the pin and simply tuck the long end through the loop you've created just like you would with a normal tie.

How to tie a bow tie

Drape the tie around your neck and cross one end over the other, making sure one end is slightly longer than the other.

Bring the long end up through the loop you've created.

Double the short end over itself to create the front base loop of the bow tie. Drop the long end down over this base loop.

While holding everything in place, double the long end back on itself to create the second loop of the bow tie. Then poke it through the loop behind the bow tie.

Adjust the bow tie by tugging at the ends and straightening the central knot. Don't worry if it's not perfectly symmetrical. All the best bow ties are ever so slightly askew. It proves that they're not clip-ons.

The best (dressed) woman

If you are the best woman it is very important to liaise with the bride, as well as the groom, about what you should wear. You will play a prominent role on the day and feature in many of the photographs, but remember that it is the bride who should be the most noticed female on the day. So be sensitive to her feelings and discuss with her what you should wear. She may want your outfit to coordinate with the bridesmaids or other members of the wedding party.

party to wear suits they already own and simply hire matching ties or waistcoats.

If all of the guys are going to be dressed in hired or bought suits, it is safest if you all get fitted out together. It may seem like a fun idea to surprise everyone by hiring bright pink tails and matching top hat, but rest assured, in the cold grey light of the wedding morning you'll suddenly realize that you're going to look pretty idiotic. Don't forget that your get-up will be preserved for all time in the wedding photos. The bride and groom are supposed to be the centre of attention, not you.

Oh, and talking of top hats – unless you're royalty (or a magician with a pet rabbit) then my advice would be, don't bother. They just look pompous. If the groom seems keen on hiring them then, as a good friend, you should do everything in your power to dissuade him from this fashion faux pas. You'll end up carrying it around all day and losing it; or else Auntie Joan will inadvertently sit on it.

If the clothing is being hired you should go with the groom the week before the wedding and help him to pick everything up and ensure that it finds its way to the correct member of the wedding party. Get everyone to try it on before the big day to avoid mix-ups.

A wedding is one of the few occasions in your lifetime where you may be required to wear a cravat. (Unless of course you fancy yourself as something of a Regency dandy.) Chances are that none of the ushers or the groom will know how to tie one, so it's your job to make sure that you do. (See the box opposite to learn the easiest way to tie one properly.)

At some weddings, especially those that have an evening reception, you may be required to wear black tie. Clip-on or band bow ties are the worst. You have to go for a proper bow tie. (See page 40 for how to tie it with style.)

Your gift

Amid all the chaos it's easy to forget that you too need to buy a wedding present and card for the happy couple. As best man your present should really be something special. You are honoured to be best friend to the groom and you ought to repay that honour by choosing a gift he and his wife will treasure.

The easiest option is to go for one of the more individual items on the wedding list (if the couple have one). But if you really want to make an impact, why not find out from them if there's something special that doesn't appear on the list? Or perhaps you can think of something yourself that will have special significance? Give your gift and card to the couple a few days before the wedding.

Organize the ushers

Even if your groom has appointed a chief usher you are ultimately in charge, so you should make sure they all know what they have to do. Although they are there to generally help out, the ushers have three main tasks:

To guide the guests into their seats at the wedding venue and hand out order of ceremony sheets. (See Seating the guests, pages 53–5.)

To direct drivers into parking spaces at both the wedding and reception venues.

To provide guests with directions to the reception venue. (See Direct people to the reception, page 60.)

Compile a list of their tasks and add any other relevant notes that they may find useful. If you think it will help, send them the list in advance so that they can take a look over it. Check that you still have all the ushers' mobile phone numbers in your phone from the stag party. Oh, and don't worry about the useless usher. You're bound to have one – every wedding does. Just be sure to give him a duty that he can't screw up too badly. Directing car parking isn't usually too taxing.

The ring

Yes, it's the ultimate marriage cliché: the lost wedding ring. More film footage and TV airtime is given to this particular scenario than any other part of the wedding. Insurance companies even offer policies now to cover this awful incident. And that's because it can and does happen. As best man you play a crucial part in ensuring it doesn't. First of all, check the groom has actually bought the ring well before the wedding day (three or four weeks is safe enough, and the bride usually has this task well in hand). See that he keeps it somewhere safe. The night before the wedding, make sure he doesn't go to bed without proving to you that he has it. Just to be on the safe side, keep a dress ring in your suit pocket for emergencies. A Hula Hoop will suffice if you're really desperate. (Apparently, even if it's edible it's still technically legal.)

Sometimes the best man is also required to keep hold of the bride's ring for the groom, although this duty is increasingly being handed over to the chief bridesmaid. Check with the bride whether she wants you to be in charge of both rings. Alternatively a small bridesmaid or pageboy may have been designated to carry the rings on a cushion as the bride progresses up the aisle. In this case you will need to take the cushion with you and hand it and the rings to one of the ushers at the door when the bride's attendants arrive. Remember to retrieve the rings when they arrive at the altar.

Groom's honeymoon preparations

Bogged down in all the wedding preparations, the groom often forgets that things have to be organized for the honeymoon. It's worth checking with the groom that he hasn't overlooked any honeymoon preparations such as tickets, passports, visas, etc.

A cautionary tale

Do you remember seeing in the news the story of the newly-weds who booked a honeymoon to Sydney in Australia? They reserved the flights through a website, paid for the tickets and happily boarded the plane the day after their wedding. When the pilot announced that their flight was bound for Montreal in Canada, the hapless couple simply assumed that this was the first fuelling stop on the way to Australia. It wasn't until they had boarded their connecting flight – to Nova Scotia – that the penny finally dropped: there are two Sydneys – one on the east coast of Australia and one on the east coast of Canada. Needless to say, there were no opera houses or beach barbecues where they ended up.

Order of ceremony and wedding day schedule

An order of ceremony usually has the name of the bride and groom, date and the name of the wedding venue on the front. Inside it will list the different stages of the ceremony, as well as the words of any readings, hymns and prayers. Sometimes the best man, ushers, bridesmaids and pageboys are credited too. If there is to be an order of ceremony sheet, it's often the duty of the best man to pick them up from the bride. Consult with the bride and arrange a convenient time with her, it's usually about a week before the wedding. Keep them in a safe place and obviously you need to remember to take them with you to the wedding venue. Depending on where and when the wedding is going to take place, you might be able to leave them at the wedding venue when you attend the rehearsal, but don't do this unless you are absolutely sure that they won't be moved or thrown away by accident.

There can be dozens of different instalments to a modern wedding that need to be organized with military precision, so most couples now also compile a wedding schedule with instructions for the best man, the ushers and the bridesmaids. You should arm yourself with several copies of this schedule as everyone involved will look to you to tell them what happens, where it happens and when. If you don't have a detailed schedule then chaos is bound to ensue. The bride and groom should print up a schedule a few days before the wedding. Help them to get this right.

The rehearsal

All the best public performances are preceded by a dress rehearsal. Weddings are no exception. This is a chance for everyone involved to iron out any last-minute problems and to ensure that everything goes swimmingly on the big day. The rehearsal is generally held one or two days before the wedding.

The main purpose of the rehearsal is to do a brief walk through of the actual ceremony so that all the members of the wedding party know exactly what they're supposed to do, where they have to stand and when to kneel or sit. Note that you're not required to wear your full wedding outfit to the rehearsal.

In addition to the run through, the rehearsal is an opportunity for you to familiarize yourself with the wedding venue and to check that the timing of the schedule and itinerary is realistic. The ushers should attend the rehearsal as well and this will give you the chance to confirm that they all know exactly what they're supposed to be doing. You'll also be able to reassure the groom, the bride and their families that you really are the right man for the job and that you're on top of things. Although if they still have any doubts at this late stage then perhaps you've been a little remiss in your earlier duties. This is the time for you to really shine.

Use this time to get to know the layout of the venue. Find out where the toilets are (I guarantee you'll be asked) and where everyone is supposed to park their cars on the big day. Memorize exactly where everyone is supposed to sit, stand and speak. Above all, make certain that your opinion of what your duties are coincides exactly with the opinions of the groom, bride and their families. A good rule of thumb is simply to pay attention and do what you're told. At this late stage you will do no one any favours if you criticize the proceedings, however constructive you think your criticisms may be. Keep your suggestions to yourself and go with the flow. You have to see the wedding as a huge broth with far too many cooks trying to stir it. The list of these cooks is a long and distinguished one: the bride is on it; the groom may throw in a few wise words (but his voice will almost certainly be drowned out by the bride's); the bride's mother will have an opinion on everything; so might the groom's mother; then perhaps there's the wedding planner. People you won't find on this list are the father of the bride (even though he's probably foregoing his pension to pay for the reception), the father of the groom, and you, the best man. Just button your lip. Believe me, it'll be much better in the long run.

Whoever has been chosen to marry the couple – be it a vicar, a rabbi, a priest, a mullah, a registrar, a humanist or a druid, it's likely that he or she will want to run a pretty tight ship. No one wants the wedding from hell. No one wants to end up being featured on *You've Been Framed*, least of all the person officiating at the ceremony. He or she is a professional doing a job and should be treated with respect. The rehearsal will probably be your first chance to meet this official. Pay attention and try to establish a connection. This will help things run more smoothly at the main event. The rehearsal and the ceremony are not the places to clown around. That can wait until the reception.

What to bring on the day

Check off the items on this list:

☐ Suit	☐ Handkerchief
☐ Waistcoat	☐ Umbrella
☐ Shirt	☐ Cash
☐ Socks	☐ Speech cue cards
☐ Shoes	☐ Letters/cards from absent friends
☐ Cufflinks	☐ Order of ceremony sheets
☐ Tie	and wedding schedule
☐ Underwear	☐ Paperwork (licence, etc.)
☐ Belt	☐ Oops! Nearly forgot – the ring.

There's a famous Hollywood adage which says 'Never work with children or animals'. Fortunately very few weddings feature our furry friends. But it's likely that if there are pageboys or bridesmaids at least one will be under the age of five. Little kids can be funny and little kids can be sweet. But a tantrum is never far away. Fortunately, as best man you won't be expected to deal with such a situation – unless of course the kid in question is yours. But you may be called upon to help out at some stage. Just be prepared. Make sure you know the kids' names, who their mums and dads are and most importantly, where they are. Keep a couple of sweets in your jacket pocket – they are the ultimate quick cure for tears and tantrums. If, for whatever bizarre reason, animals are involved, make sure that someone, ideally their owner or handler, is responsible for looking (and cleaning up) after them.

The rehearsal dinner

The rehearsal dinner is an established tradition in the USA, and is one that is becoming increasingly popular in the UK. It used to be strictly an immediate family affair, plus perhaps the best man. But it is becoming more common for other family members, especially those who are travelling long distances to the wedding, plus ushers to be invited to attend.

By this stage all the hiccups will have been ironed out and the bride, groom and their families will be confident after the rehearsal. You too should have assuaged any worries you might have had. In any case, there's very little you can do this late in the day. Just relax, and look forward to the event you have been building up to.

Since you'll be making the main speech on the big day, you won't be expected to stand up and speak at the rehearsal dinner. But it's best to have a few words prepared just in case – even if it's just a few best wishes and a toast.

Oh, and don't overdo it on the booze. No one wants a best man with a hangover. Key decisions tend to go wrong. You should have done all your drinking at the stag party. Make your excuses and get yourself an early night. You can let your hair down after you've discharged all your best man duties.

Messages from absent friends

In the old days people who were unable to attend the wedding used to send telegrams. Nowadays it's more likely to be letters, cards or emails. Whatever the medium, it's your responsibility to read out messages from absent friends during your speech, so remember to pick these up from the bride's family the day before the wedding.

The night before the big day

Depending on where the wedding is taking place and the arrangements that you've made, you may or may not be staying in the same place as the groom on the night before the wedding. If you're not staying in the same place and you're not going to see him, make sure you give him a call to check that he's okay and that he's set his alarm clock. Preferably two alarm clocks.

If you're staying in the same place, don't stay up talking half the night and don't drink too much. Use your time together productively and check that you have everything that you need for the big day. It will be less to worry about on the day itself.

Chapter Five

The Big Day

Today is the day you really cannot afford to make any mistakes. Follow this guide and hopefully you won't. Weddings attract the unexpected, which is usually what makes them memorable, so do be prepared to think on your feet. Lots of cash in your pocket, a clean handkerchief and a fully charged mobile phone should be weapons enough to see off most wedding day disasters. Give yourself the best chance to do the best job you possibly can. Go to bed early the night before, get a good night's sleep and rise early on the morning of the big day.

This timeline is for a mid-afternoon wedding. Use this as a guide to work out your own schedule for a wedding earlier or later in the day.

8.00 a.m.

◆ Wake up to your alarm clock. Today is not a day for a lie-in.

8.05 a.m.

◆ Wake up the groom. If you're not staying with him then phone him to wake him. (Increasingly, nowadays, best man and groom stay in the same hotel, or at the groom's place, the night before the wedding. It makes getting to the wedding venue on time a lot easier.)

8.10 a.m.

◆ Check the groom hasn't gone back to sleep.

8.15 a.m.

◆ Phone the chief usher to check he has everything under control.

8.20 a.m.

◆ Last-minute check of travel arrangements. Make sure you and the groom have something to eat before leaving, even if you don't feel like it.

9.00 a.m.

◆ Check you have all the clothing, accessories, money and paperwork (licence or certificate of banns) you need. And for goodness sake remember the ring(s). (See What to bring on the day, page 46.)

Morning

◆ Collect buttonholes (and order of ceremony sheets if you haven't collected them already) from the bride.

3 hours to go

◆ Best man, groom and all the ushers meet up at the wedding venue. If you have to travel far to the wedding venue, always allow some extra journey time. Sod's Law dictates that traffic jams and engine problems are rife on wedding days. Check that you have the ring(s). Carry out any last minute checks.

2 hours to go

◆ All proceed to the nearest pub for the ceremonial spot of prenuptial Dutch courage (see Premarital drink, pages 52–3).

1 hour to go

◆ Get to the venue and prepare to meet, greet and seat the guests as they arrive.

10 minutes to go

◆ Check you have the ring(s). There's still time to find an emergency ring if a real one has gone astray.

5 minutes to go

◆ Take your position alongside the groom at the front of the venue.

Keep the groom calm

Any sane man this close to getting married may start to get a little apprehensive at this stage. A mild panic may even have set in. You've got to be there to stave off these emotions. First of all you have to keep calm yourself. Imagine you are an air steward on an aeroplane and the groom is a passenger sitting on the row opposite your jump seat. If the engine starts to make funny noises and you display any apprehension, he will start to worry too. But if you keep cool under pressure, then hopefully so will he.

There may of course come a time when, despite your best intentions, the wings simply fall off the plane. This is when you become something of a counsellor for the groom. Keep reassuring him that everything will be okay. Get him to the ceremony on time and with as little stress as possible. You should be able to shield him from as many of the anxieties and tensions of the wedding day as you can so that he can focus on his main task: marrying his wife.

Transport

It's likely you'll travel with the groom to the wedding venue on the morning of the big day. Better still, why not stay at his place the night before so that you can get him up and dressed in time? Aside from the stag night, this is the one time when you may have to mother the groom. It's possible his mind will be a jumble of nerves and his legs will be like jelly. You're his right-hand man and that may mean you'll have to help get him up and dressed, bundle him into the car and manhandle him to the wedding venue. Don't underestimate the effects that marriage stress can have on a man.

Transport is crucial at this stage. Do not even consider taking public transport to the wedding. Fellow travellers will cry with laughter when they spot you and the groom dressed up to the nines, stuck in traffic on a bus. You will cry with shame. Travel by car or taxi and plan to arrive at the wedding venue at least an hour and a half before everyone else. You'll need the spare time for any last minute problems and of course you'll want to meet all the ushers in the pub for a swift pint of Dutch courage prior to the ceremony (see Premarital drink, pages 52–3). Always have a taxi firm on standby in case your car doesn't make it. You'll get some funny looks if you and the groom end up having to thumb a lift in your morning suits on the edge of the motorway.

Buttonholes

It's the bride who normally orders the buttonholes for her husband-to-be and his wedding party, along with the other numerous wedding flora. As best man it's your duty to get these buttonholes from her and onto your lapel and those of the groom and ushers. Among all the other things you have to remember on the big day it may seem like just a trivial detail, but for the bride and her family it's important. Besides, if everyone is in morning suits then the buttonholes may be the only sign that you and the ushers are more than normal guests. You'll find that some guests will use the buttonholes to pick you out when they have questions to ask. Flowers are better than name tags and will be appreciated by the more short-sighted members of the wedding party.

Help the bride's family

There are always last-minute emergencies and they normally involve something crucial like the cake or the marquee. Let the bride's parents know that, if needed, you are available to save the day.

I once heard about one best man who was roped into delivering a grandmother to the church on the wedding day because no one else had the time. The nonagenarian lived quite a distance from the ceremony and when the family phoned her on the morning of the big day she had completely forgotten about it. Best man was duly dispatched to pick her up, bundle her into his car and drive her post-haste to the church. He was hailed as a saviour by the bride and her family.

Premarital drink

This has become something of a tradition in recent years. Always try to build in enough time before the ceremony actually starts so that

you and all the ushers can share a drink in a local pub with
the groom. It is, after all, his final beverage as a free man
and he will want to savour it with his closest friends.

It is also a chance to run over any last minute organizational
details and to indulge in a bit of gallows humour at the groom's
expense. In any case, what groom could even contemplate getting
married on an empty stomach? Of all the types of courage he needs,
Dutch courage is one of the most useful. Since no one, least of all
the registrar or the bride, will appreciate slurred vows, limit the
groom to just the one drink. In fact, that rule applies to everyone.

The ceremony

Seating the guests

The best man doesn't usually usher guests to their seats. His
position is beside the groom. But he will have to ensure that the
ushers know exactly what they have to do. At a formal wedding as
the guests arrive ushers should hand them an order of ceremony
sheet and direct them to the relevant side of the marriage venue.
Traditionally, friends of the bride sit on the left-hand side of the
venue and friends of the groom on the right-hand side. Nowadays,
however, couples have often known each other for years before they
get married and therefore have a lot of mutual friends. When this is
the situation guests tend to mingle on both sides. Besides, it's often
the case that the bride invites more people than the groom. If her
father is paying for the wedding he may well have exercised his
prerogative and invited a lot more of his own friends. If one side of
the venue is full and the other empty, it can look a bit odd. Ushers
should use their common sense and try to keep both sides of the
venue evenly balanced.

There are, however, certain key spots in the seating plan that
need to be reserved. At a recent wedding I went to the ushers forgot
to keep places free at the front of the church for the bride's family,
all of whom arrived late. There were a few embarrassed looks as
the mother of the bride and the ushers were forced to relocate
some of the guests to the back of the church. Here's a tip: always

---

Seating plan

For a formal wedding here is the traditional seating plan:

Left	Right
Bride's parents	Groom and best man
Bride's family and bridesmaids	Groom's parents
Bride's other relatives	Groom's close family
	Groom's other relatives
Bride's friends	Groom's friends
Ushers	Ushers

---

fill the marriage venue from the back. Save the first few rows at the front for family members. The problem is that the ushers won't necessarily know who is family and who isn't. This is why they need to ask two questions to each guest on arrival: 'Are you friends or family?'; 'Bride or groom?' If someone answers 'I'm friends with both bride and groom' then seat them on the groom's side. This will help balance numbers if the bride has invited more guests.

At very formal weddings ushers may be expected to offer their arms to female guests and escort them to their seats. If the female guest is accompanied by a man then he would follow along behind. Some women will enjoy this courtesy while others may feel uncomfortable at all the fuss. As the guests continue to arrive the ushers will quickly learn to gauge the situation.

Ushers

Here are a few tips to give to your ushers:

At all times act courteously and speak calmly with clear instructions.

Try to seat old and vulnerable guests in the coolest part of the building. A summer wedding party with 150 people in formal dress will soon heat up a venue to an uncomfortable level. You don't want guests to snore or faint during the ceremony.

If a lot of guests arrive at the same time, speed up the proceedings by allowing them to seat themselves.

You don't need to accompany every female guest to her seat. Concentrate on the older ones and any that arrive alone. Don't walk too fast – stiletto heels tend to get stuck in church-floor grates. Elderly guests may welcome a supportive arm to lean on.

After the ceremony ushers should check the wedding venue for lost property. Ladies' hats in particular tend to go astray. (I remember being an usher at one wedding where someone had left a wedding gift under one of the church pews.)

Waiting with the groom

Be prepared to wait for quite a while for the bride to arrive – it's traditional for her to be late. During this time you should be giving the groom all the moral support he needs. This could well be his most vulnerable hour, the period when he finds himself more nervous than he has ever been since he first proposed.

You won't have to stand at the front of the wedding venue with him for the entire period that you are waiting for the bride. Ushers should have been appointed to act as lookouts so that they can give you the signal the moment the bride arrives, although the arrival of her mother and the bridesmaids is an early warning that she's on her way. Normally when you get this signal, you and the groom will take your positions at the front of the venue, opposite the clergyman or the registrar, in readiness for the bride and her father.

This is often when the extreme anxiety kicks in. A groom who has up until now been cool, calm and collected, may suddenly realize the gravity of his situation, just as the bride makes her entrance. As best man, you've got to hold it all together for yourself and for your groom. If you need to mutter reassuring words under your breath to him then don't be afraid to do so. You will quite literally be his right-hand man, standing just to his right side. Do whatever is required to keep him focused and calm: act casual, whisper kind words, or even try to take his mind off the seriousness of the occasion if you need to. Just keep him cool. How many

On ceremony

You could be standing up for quite a while before and during the ceremony, and after the bride and groom, you will be the next focus of everyone's attention. Here are a few tips on how to get through the ceremony with grace:

Don't lock your knees when standing for a long time. It will restrict blood flow to your lower legs and may cause you to topple over.

Stand up straight with your feet slightly apart and keep still. Every now and then subtly shift your weight from one foot to the other. This also prevents fainting.

No nail biting, scratching, or nose picking, no matter how nervous you are. Even if there is no videographer, there will always be a guest lurking somewhere with a camcorder.

Avoid chewing gum. Little mints are much more subtle.

Smile. Even if your nerves are shot to pieces on the inside, this should be a happy day for you too.

However casual the ceremony, don't be tempted to put your hands in your pockets. By your side or clasped behind you are the only options.

The bride and groom should be your main focus of attention so that you play your part in the ceremony at the right time. Don't look around for friends or try to attract their attention. There'll be plenty of time for socializing at the reception.

You've Been Framed clips have you seen where the groom faints and keels over at the crucial moment? It happens so often that a lot of wedding officials keep smelling salts in their pockets. They claim that they're required more for grooms than for brides.

The ring

It's your job to safeguard the ring (or rings, if you're also looking after the groom's ring from the bride) until the crucial moment. Keep it in your front pocket. Don't put it on your own finger. Imagine the embarrassment if, because of nerves and heat, your fingers swell and you can't get the ring off again. You don't want to end up mutating from best man into groom do you?

Signing the register

It's normal for just the parents, the groom and the bride to sign the register. Occasionally the best man and chief bridesmaid are also asked to do this. Don't worry, it's very self-explanatory.

The procession

At a church wedding it's traditional for the best man to accompany the bridesmaids, and in particular the chief bridesmaid, out of the church after the bride and groom. All eyes will be watching you and the rest of the wedding party and the only time you'll have more cameras pointed at you is if one day you enter court on

---

Practical joke

Just like the humiliation of the groom on the stag do, wedding day practical jokes are also a nuptial tradition. What you mustn't do, however, is overdo the joke and throw the bride and groom off course or do anything to spoil their day. For most of the early part of the day they will be vulnerable souls. You'll know best how the couple will react. It's up to you to gauge whether a joke will be appreciated.

A classic trick that the best man can play is to write a message in white paint on the soles of the groom's wedding shoes, so that it's visible to the whole congregation when he kneels at the altar. 'Help' on the left sole and 'me!' on the right sole tends to work quite well.

Oh, and don't think that just because it's not you getting married that you won't be subject to a few practical jokes yourself. A friend of mine attended a Catholic wedding where the bride, groom and all the ushers had to kneel together at the altar during the ceremony. Various messages including 'I'm next', 'You think he's nervous?' and 'Help me too!' had been painted on the soles of the shoes of the best man and his ushers.

a murder charge. So make the most of it. If there are only two bridesmaids of similar ages, take one on each arm and walk slowly and calmly. Enjoy the attention and keep smiling.

If the bride's dress gets tangled, just remember it's not your job to fix it. This is the exclusive domain of the chief bridesmaid. Besides, wedding dresses are often huge, trailing affairs. You think you're being helpful but you'll only end up making things worse.

Wedding fee

This is normally the domain of the father of the bride and should have been settled well beforehand. But if payment has been overlooked you may be required to cover costs, at least temporarily. Before the wedding day, check diplomatically with the bride and groom as to who is financially responsible.

Confetti

Certain venues can be a bit sniffy about confetti, especially if it's not a variety that birds can eat or otherwise biodegradable. You may be asked to make an announcement on the subject before the ceremony starts. Many venues restrict where it can be thrown.

It's a good idea for you to provide some confetti of your own. It looks great in the photographs and if you have several packets on your person you can collude with the photographer and time your bombardment to perfection.

The tradition of throwing confetti dates back to pre-Christian times when guests showered the newly-weds with grain to symbolize fertility.

Help the photographer

The wedding photographer never knows the names of everyone he's supposed to be capturing on film, unless he's a very old family friend, in which case his photos risk being blurred and shaky.

Professional photographers need help with their task and they always look to the best man for assistance. It's a good idea if you

The no-show groom

What should you do if the groom fails to turn up?! This is another one of those Hollywood nightmare scenarios: the groom who loses his nerve at the last minute and fails to turn up for the wedding ceremony. The good news is that, as best man, unlike in the olden days, you are no longer obliged to marry the bride in his place. The bad news is that you now have no rest until you have found him. The responsibility is on your shoulders.

Get things organized quickly. Rally together a search party, using only people from the groom's side of the family. If members of the bride's family find him who knows what might happen?

Check the obvious places: his family home, his own home, his ex-girlfriend's place, the nearest airport, the pub, a high cliff. If you do find him then be sure to treat him with kid gloves. By this stage he will be a very fragile animal indeed. Thoughts of wedded bliss will be far from his mind. Instead he'll be considering emigration.

If he really has made up his mind and you can't talk him into going ahead with the marriage, then sorry, but it's your job to break it to the bride and her family. By this time their extreme rage will have developed into a desire for his blood. Since the groom is about to leave the country, it's you who will be next in the firing line. The father of the bride will be especially belligerent. His beloved daughter has just been jilted at the altar, he has been shown up in front of all his friends, and now he's got a hefty bill for a reception that no one's going to attend. In the absence of the groom, he will turn his aggression on you instead. Apologize profusely and sympathize with his situation. Don't reveal the groom's whereabouts and don't ask whether he's got a job lot of champagne he wants to sell to you. Consider boarding that plane to Brazil along with the groom.

and the snapper have a list of what shots are required. Along with the ushers you can then rally all the relevant people together and make sure the right heads are in the right photos. People will be desperate to get to the reception and get started on the champagne, so keep the photo session as painless as possible. If possible, get any large group photos out of the way first, since it may prove difficult to round everyone up later once they've started on the refreshments. Most of the photos will be very formal. Your bride and groom will be grateful if you and the ushers arrange some fun shots towards the end of the session. The bride lying across the arms of the groom, best man and all the ushers is a favourite. Throwing top hats into the air is another.

Direct people to the reception

A loud voice and an assertive manner are needed for this duty. The bride and groom will be falling over each other in post-nuptial bliss, so it's up to you to make certain that all the guests know exactly how to get to the reception.

Out of 150-odd guests there are sure to be some who can't quite make the transition from ceremony to reception. The best man is their only hope of reaching the champagne and therefore they'll latch onto you for directions.

If you have enough ushers you can position them at key turning points on the route. Arms outstretched, dressed in morning suits and adorned with buttonhole flowers, they will be more obvious than any number of signposts.

The reception

The receiving line

The receiving line is the first port of call for all the guests once they arrive at the reception. Not every wedding has one but when they do it's a chance for guests to officially meet and congratulate the bride, groom and their parents.

The traditional order of a receiving line is the bride's mother and father, the groom's parents, and the bride and groom. It's unlikely you'll be asked to actually stand in the line, but if you are, you should stand at the end with the chief bridesmaid. You'll actually be more useful directing the guests once they arrive at the reception. Guide them first to the receiving line. In the absence of one of these send them straight for the trays of bubbly. They won't need much encouragement for the latter.

Dinner seating arrangements

At a lot of weddings the best man sits at the top table with the bride, groom and their families. Chances are you'll be in such demand that you won't have time to enjoy the wine before the speeches. Don't be tempted, though. One glass is okay, but any more and you'll seriously risk messing up the speech.

Drunken guests

By no means is the best man expected to act as doorman, but you may be called upon to help if guests get out of hand. Alcohol affects different people in different ways and there are always a couple of guests who imbibe too much. If someone really is causing an embarrassment then you ought to try to remove him (and yes it is usually a man) from the reception until he has sobered up a bit. A good way of doing this is to get one of the staff to tell the offending person that he has a phone call in the main house or hotel reception. Once he has stumbled away from the reception you can collar him and politely explain that he needs to sober up. This will avoid a scene in front of all the other guests.

I heard of one particular wedding where the bride had invited one of her ex-boyfriends. Under normal circumstances this would have been okay. Unfortunately, after many glasses of champagne, circumstances were anything but normal. The ex-boyfriend got totally drunk and decided to try to reignite his relationship with the bride, much to the chagrin of her new husband. It was left to the best man to step in and sort things out. With supreme tact worthy of a Middle-Eastern diplomat he managed to guide the ex-boyfriend out of the marquee, sober him up a bit with lots of strong black coffee and finally make him see the error of his ways.

Master of ceremonies

If it's a very formal wedding there may be a toastmaster, in which case you only have to worry about your own speech. But at some weddings you may be called upon to do a bit of MC-ing. Normally this just involves making an announcement when dinner is served, ensuring that the microphone works and that the speeches take place in the correct order. More and more wedding speeches are being scheduled before the guests sit down for dinner, but conventionally they take place after dessert when the guests are drinking their coffee.

Once you and the other speakers are ready to strut your stuff, stand up and jingle a spoon in a wine glass to get everyone's attention. Introduce the first speaker. Traditionally the father or close friend of the bride opens up proceedings. His job is to thank all the guests for coming and to welcome his new son-in-law into the family. He will also reveal a few embarrassing anecdotes about the bride's early life before proposing a toast to the newly-weds.

Now it's the turn of the groom. His job is easy since the main function of his speech is to thank everyone for making the wedding day possible. This must include both sets of parents and all the guests, and possibly even the caterers and florists if they have family connections. He should then wax lyrical about the bridesmaids and of course his beautiful new wife.

Now it's crunch time. The moment of truth. Your opportunity to really shine. The best man's speech (see Part Two, pages 75–121).

Chapter Six

Final Duties

Tempting though it is to think that once you have delivered your speech you are off the hook and free to make up for lost time, just bear in mind that the wedding is not over until the bride and groom have been dispatched on their honeymoon. You still have a number of remaining duties to see to before you can finally breathe a sigh of relief and relax.

A lot of best men make the mistake of believing that once they have punctuated their speech with the final toast then their duties are complete. Not quite. You're still expected to a certain extent to be a gracious party host and to ensure everyone enjoys a great reception. You also ought to take charge of getting the couple safely away on their honeymoon. Don't miss this chance to indulge in the classic wedding tradition of decorating the honeymooners' car.

Party host

As best man, you are, in a way, one of the hosts of the wedding reception. Once you've delivered your speech it's then part of your job to keep the party going. You'll certainly be expected to dance with the chief bridesmaid, to get up on the dancefloor early and to encourage everyone else to join in. You may need to give direction to the band or the DJ. You have a responsibility for ensuring that everyone has a good time. Saying that, don't deny yourself a few drinks. By this stage you will very much deserve them.

Why do we tie things to the couple's car?

This tradition harks all the way back to ancient Egypt. When Egyptian traders clinched a deal they used to exchange sandals with one another as a sign that goods had been transferred from one person to another. When a girl married her new husband, the bride's father would give the groom his sandals, to signify that his daughter was now his property. (There was of course no such thing as sexual equality in ancient times.)

The Romans took the tradition one step further and used to throw shoes over the happy couple at the end of the wedding ceremony. This was gradually modified over the centuries until it became customary to tie shoes to the back of the wedding carriage, and later the motor car, as the newly-weds drove away.

In the final evolution of the tradition shoes were replaced with tin cans. Much cheaper than Jimmy Choos.

Getting the couple away

Long gone are the days when the married couple would depart from the reception after dinner, leaving their guests to enjoy the party without them. These days the bride and groom are expected to be the life and soul of the party all the way until the end of the evening, and may indeed be determined not to miss a minute of the whole experience. With so many big weddings taking place in marquees, they may even be hosting a lunch the following day.

Eventually the time will come when they head off on their honeymoon. Your last duty as best man is to see that their final transition into married life goes smoothly. Help them get their honeymoon bags packed into the car. Take charge of any clothing the groom may have hired and ensure it gets back to the hire shop. And promise the newly-weds that you will see any presents left over from the wedding safely home. If you live nearby, offer to take care of their house while they are away. It would be a generous touch to get some basic supplies in and pop a bottle of champagne in the fridge for when they get back home.

Decorate the car

As best man, you should help decorate their car. The old but very effective cliché is to tie tin cans to the rear bumper or spray 'Just Married' across the rear windscreen. Festering kippers under the bonnet used to be an old favourite, too. A safer option, though, is to tie streamers to the wing mirrors and balloons to the aerial.

Bride and groom will love the attention as they drive off from the reception knowing that everyone they pass on the road will know they are newly-weds. It's one of the more romantic episodes in a typical wedding day – why do you think it has featured in so many films over the years? Oh, and it makes for great photos, too. But remember – it's not funny to interfere with the mechanics of the car. Bride and groom may have a plane to catch.

If the couple are staying the night locally before embarking on their honeymoon, a hotel room practical joke may be in order. This may range from the safe option of confetti in the bedclothes to the slightly more risky cling film stretched over the toilet seat. Again, use your judgement as to whether a joke will go down well or not. Once you've waved them off, pour yourself a well-earned drink.

At the end of the day

Before you can call it a day, be sure to offer your help to the bride's and groom's parents – they may need assistance clearing up, loading the car and making sure that stragglers go home.

Congratulations,
you have succeeded in your role as best man!

Chapter Seven

Wedding Customs

Every nation, culture and religion has its own take on the wedding ceremony and the party afterwards. Civil weddings last just a few minutes while Catholic ceremonies can go on for several hours. In India you're lucky to get the whole thing over in less than a week. In today's multicultural society you may well be asked to be best man at a wedding where the customs are totally unfamiliar to you.

The bride and groom may be of different nationalities or from different faiths and wish to combine elements of both. The bride and groom will brief you as to your duties and tell you everything you need to know. You should respect any traditions that are called for. This chapter also covers same-sex and double weddings.

Catholic weddings

There are two types of Roman Catholic wedding: a simple ceremony and a full nuptial mass. For the latter, which lasts longer since it includes holy communion, bride and groom must both be Catholic. As well as a ring, the groom gives gold and silver to his bride as a symbol of his worldly goods.

Jewish weddings

The ceremony takes place in a synagogue, normally underneath a canopy decorated with flowers. If it's Orthodox, male and female guests sit on opposite sides and cover their heads. After the vows have been exchanged the couple sip wine from the same glass and the groom will then break the glass under the heel of his shoe. As best man you will probably be asked to sign as a witness to the licence. Also, a point to note is that it is not traditional for the best man to make a speech at a Jewish wedding.

Muslim weddings

Many Muslims hold a wedding over several days but the ritual itself is a fairly simple affair.

The bride and groom are in separate rooms where they may or may not be able to see one other, depending on how conservative the families are. An officiant, familiar with Islamic law, heads to each room separately and asks both the bride and groom if they consent to the marriage. The couple then sign the marriage contract while witnesses look on. Finally the officiant brings the bride and groom together and pronounces them husband and wife.

Before and after the actual marriage there are many different traditional ceremonies, depending on which Muslim country the couple lives in.

Having a best man is not a custom at a traditional Muslim wedding. On the wedding day a procession of the groom's friends and family accompany him to the wedding venue.

Civil weddings

If this is held in a registry office it will be a very simple affair and may be restricted to a small number of guests. If it is held in a larger licensed venue, such as a civic hall or a historic building, then it could have all the pomp of a religious wedding but without the religious language or ritual.

Double weddings

Not surprisingly, very few brides are willing to share the limelight with another bride on their special day unless it's her twin sister and they do everything together. That's why double weddings would normally only feature siblings, where some of the guests are already mutual to two of the parties involved.

Each groom will have his own best man and each best man will act pretty much the same as if it was a single wedding. If you find yourself best man at a double wedding it's crucial you meet up with your counterpart well before the ceremony to share notes.

In the case of two sisters it's traditional for the eldest bride and her bridesmaids to walk down the aisle first. If the brides aren't sisters then the bride with the older groom normally takes precedence over the bride with the younger groom.

Gay weddings

A lot of Western countries are starting to relax the laws on same-sex marriages. Since traditionally there are no set procedures for gay weddings, couples can come up with their own ideas. When two men are tying the knot you'd expect a best man and when there are two women getting married you'd expect a best woman. There are no hard and fast rules governing this, however. Some gay weddings feature two best men or women, with each person in the couple having chosen someone as a supporter. Otherwise the ceremony pretty much follows the conventions of a civil wedding. There are very few religions around the world yet progressive enough to allow gay weddings in their churches.

Wedding traditions

The world is a small place, so you may find yourself the best man at a wedding in a foreign country. Every country has its own quirky wedding traditions. Here are some of the more interesting ones.

Armenia
At a traditional Armenian church wedding the best man is called the 'brother of the cross' because he holds up a cross during the ceremony. At the reception the guests throw coins at the bride.

China
Chinese brides will often change their wedding dress at least three times during the day. The bride also serves tea to the groom's parents during the formal ceremony, which is only attended by the couple's immediate family.

Croatia
Wedding guests walk three times around a well and then throw apples into it. This symbolizes the fertility of the newly-weds.

Cyprus
Guests pin money to the bride and groom during the first dance.

Czech Republic
Before the ceremony a baby is placed on the couple's bed to encourage fertility.

Denmark
An arch of pine branches is erected around the front door of the bride's family home. During the reception, guests will cut the groom's tie and socks with scissors.

Estonia
The Estonians have a tradition for predicting which bachelor guest will be the next to get married. They blindfold the groom and whichever head he places his top hat on will be the next to marry.

Finland
The bride's mother-in-law puts a plate on the bride's head at the start of the wedding dance. When the plate falls the number of broken pieces represent how many children the couple will have.

Greece
Along with the priest, the best man is in charge of the ceremony. He places gold crowns or wreaths made of orange blossoms on the head of the bride and groom. Plates are smashed on the floor during the reception.

Hungary
If male guests dance with the bride and give her coins then she kisses them in return.

India
The day before the ceremony the bride will have her hands and feet decorated with henna paint. After the formal vows the groom's father or brother showers them with flower petals, then, holding a coconut above their heads, circles the newly-weds three times.

Indonesia
Everyone who even vaguely knows the bride or groom is invited to an Indonesian wedding. There can often be thousands of guests. It is considered rude to be invited to the reception but not attend.

Iran
After the ceremony the bride and groom will have shavings of sugar dropped onto their heads.

Japan
The bride wears a hood on her kimono to hide what are called her 'horns of jealousy' from her future mother-in-law. The bride and groom drink nine cups of sake during the ritual, after which they are considered united. More sake is then drunk by all present to symbolize the bonding of the couple and their families.

Korea
The groom's father throws red dates at the bride in order to help her become fertile. Ducks and geese are often included in the ceremony as they symbolize faithfulness.

Latvia
The ushers often pretend to kidnap the bride at a Latvian wedding. The groom then has to buy a round of drinks to win her back.

Malaysia
Each guest receives a hard-boiled egg which symbolizes the fertility of the married couple. Trays of food given as wedding gifts are sometimes decorated with origami flowers or cranes folded from paper money.

Morocco
After the wedding the bride walks around her new house three times before she crosses the threshold.

Norway
Whenever the groom leaves the room during the reception, all the single men queue up to kiss the bride in his absence. It also works the other way; when the bride leaves, all the single women kiss the groom.

Pakistan
Weddings last four days with the actual ceremony on the third day. The bride does not see her husband until the ceremony.

Poland
It is considered lucky if a Polish bride drinks from a ceremonial glass of wine without spilling a drop.

Russia
After the toasts, guests throw their champagne glasses on the floor. It's good luck if they break.

South Africa
A traditional church ceremony may include the twelve symbols of African life. These are wheat, wine, water, pepper, salt, herbs, honey, a pot and spoon, a spear, a shield, a broom and a copy of the Bible or the Koran.

Sudan
The mother of the bride welcomes the groom to the venue with a garland of flowers. After the wedding the newly-weds break an egg before entering their new home.

Sweden
Just before the bride gets married her parents give her a silver and a gold coin. She puts one in each shoe.

Thailand
Thai ceremonies are conducted by the oldest relative of the couple, following a blessing from Bhuddist monks. Bride, groom and guests dip their hands in a conch shell full of water for good luck.

Tibet
The bride is taken on a white horse to the groom's house, where the ceremony takes place. Bride and groom are given ceremonial scarves to wear around their necks. Sometimes there are so many that they can't look down to see their feet.

THE SPEECH

'When a man is asked to make a speech, the first
thing he has to decide is what to say.'

Gerald Ford
US President

Chapter Eight

Basic Structure

This is the moment you've really been preparing for. It's the one best man's duty that you will most be remembered for. And this is very probably the part of the day you have most been dreading. Fear not, however. This section provides you with a basic speech structure that you can either follow exactly, or adapt and change as you see fit.

My brother has been best man three times. The first time he was so nervous about his speech he used to wake up in the middle of the night with nightmares. And that was three months before the big day. The second time he was a bit more relaxed. He'd been through it once before and knew what to expect. The third time it was a breeze. Without any doubt, the key to making a great speech is to be thorough in your preparation.

Whatever you do and however accustomed you are to public speaking do NOT try to wing it on the day. You're going to be standing up in front of possibly 150 or more people, many of them strangers. You're probably going to be wearing a hot, formal suit. You're expected to be courteous, grateful, full of praise and funny. On the outside you've got to look smart, confident and in control. However, it's very likely that on the inside your nerves will be completely shot to pieces.

There are three stages to any great speech: writing, practising and delivering. Even if you're the most nervous public speaker in the world, provided you take heed of the following advice, I can guarantee you'll be able to present a heartfelt and witty speech that all the guests and especially the bride and groom are bound to remember – for all the right reasons, that is. Traditionally the father of the bride speaks first, followed by the groom, and then it's your turn to shine.

How the speech should run

You're free to deliver the key elements of your speech in any order you like. But there should be a logical progression to what you say. Here is a fail-safe structure.

❈ **Great opening line**
   Get things going with an unforgettable opening line. Make your audience laugh and they'll be on your side right from the start. (See Great opening lines, pages 86–9.)

❈ **Thanks and a joke**
   Thank both the father of the bride and the groom for their

speeches. Sound sincere when you do this, even if one of
the speeches was a stinker.

As best man, it's not your official duty to thank the parents
of the bride and all the other contributors who helped with the
wedding. However, just to be on the safe side, why not throw
in a few well meant words of gratitude?

Now make a joke about how the groom is soon to have his
character well and truly assassinated. There's nothing wrong with
instilling a bit of fear in him. You want the guests to be full of
anticipation and the groom to be full of dread about what you
are about to reveal.

❄ Reply on behalf of the bridesmaids

Your traditional role as best man is to reply to the groom on
behalf of all the bridesmaids. You don't need to be too formal
about this, but you must remind everyone how beautiful they
all look. They have spent hours in front of the mirror and have
endured weeks of dress fittings. A throwaway remark about how
nice they look isn't enough. You've really got to wax lyrical about
their beauty. Try to sound genuine rather than sycophantic. Give
the younger members of the bridal party a mention, too.

❄ Congratulate the newly-weds

Give your congratulations to the newly-weds. As with so much
of the best man's speech there's a fine line between sounding
sincere and cheesy. You don't need to employ nauseating lovey-
dovey language. However professionally you deliver cheesy
words, they will always sound cheesy. It's far better to come
up with a few simple, well-meant tidings.

Look at the couple fondly as you congratulate them. They
and everyone else will notice the expression in your face as
you do this and realize the message is coming from your heart.
And remember to tell them how honoured you are to have been
chosen as best man.

If you do end up sounding too schmaltzy you can always try
ending your congratulations with a few marriage witticisms:

'[Bride], treat him just like a pet dog – plenty of
exercise, lots of affection, three meals a day and
a loose lead.'

'[Groom], make sure you cuddle and kiss her daily.
And if her daily won't agree to it, try the au pair!'

❋ Compliment the bride

Although compliments to the bride are not an official part
of your speech duty, a line about how beautiful the bride looks
will always be appreciated. This will also encourage the guests
who will clap and cheer in support after you say it.

❋ The groom's in safe hands

Now you can talk about how the groom is in very safe hands
with his new bride. It's an opportunity for you to describe to
everyone how utterly useless the groom is around the house
and at looking after himself. Try the following:

'Around the house, [groom] is like God Himself. He's
never seen, he thinks he's the holy of holies and if he
even so much as lifts a finger it's considered a bloody
miracle.'

'[Groom] is extremely responsible indeed. If anything
ever goes wrong you can be sure that it's him who's
responsible.

But be sure it's only the groom you mock. Whatever you do,
don't take the mickey out of the bride.

❋ Mock the groom

At this juncture you can go on the offensive. This is your chance
to really make fun of the groom and in the process make your
audience laugh. However, the humour should always be
affectionate and playful.

Perhaps pick on a particular aspect of the groom's character
and expose it for the benefit of everyone present. (See Subjects

to avoid, pages 89–91 and Safe joke material pages 91–2.)
If the groom is renowned for being forgetful:

> '[Groom] doesn't know the meaning of the word
> forgetful. Mind you, there are loads of words he
> doesn't know the meaning of.'

If the groom's a bit slow on the uptake:

> 'In all the many years I've known [groom], no one
> has ever questioned his intelligence. In fact, come to
> think of it, I don't think I've ever heard anyone even
> mention it.'

If the groom is bad at DIY:

> '[Groom] has been described as awkward, bumbling
> and cack-handed. Let's face it – a mother should
> know these things.'

If the groom is lazy:

> '[Groom] is a very lucky man. His job allows him to
> work eight hours and sleep eight hours. Unfortunately
> they tend to be the same eight hours.'

❊ Praise the groom

Always balance these jokes by following them with some serious
and poignant stuff. Remember you're there to praise the groom
as well as ridicule him in front of family and friends. You are,
after all, his best man. Tell everyone what a great friend he is to
you and remind everyone what a terrific bloke he is. Everyone
has a heroic moment in their past you can embarrass them with.

If you're worried it's all starting to sound a bit cheesy you can
always follow it with a playful put-down.

Try this:

> 'Just take a look at the groom. What a wonderful man
> he is. [Pause.] Maybe we can cryogenically freeze him
> until scientists find a cure.'

Or:

> '[Groom's] so unique that it's almost impossible to
> forget him. But, believe me, it's well worth the effort.'

Anecdotes

Now it's time for all the anecdotes and funny stories you have
prepared (see Ideas, pages 93–4). The guests will love being
entertained by the antics, capers and various scrapes that the
groom has been involved in over the years. Use these tales to
paint a picture of his character and get lots of laughs from the
guests. Embellishment and exaggeration is perfectly acceptable;
to be expected even.

One thing you must be sure not to do is alienate your
listeners with in-jokes and obscure stories that they can't relate
to. A 10-minute story hinting at events which took place on the
stag do may have all the ushers in stitches, but the rest of the
wedding guests won't understand and won't be interested.
Try to keep it relevant to everyone if you can. And don't be
too cruel to the groom (see Subjects to avoid, pages 89–91).

Heartfelt wishes

In your efforts to make everyone laugh, don't forget that your
speech should include some emotional stuff. If you feel you
may have overdone the ridiculing then you can always throw
in something about how lucky the groom is and what a perfect
couple the newly-weds are. By alternating funny stuff with
heartfelt stuff you ensure that your speech remains balanced.

Messages from absentees

Now's the time to read out any messages from guests who
couldn't make it to the wedding. If there are no absentees,
why not include a few fabricated messages, just for a laugh?

> 'Dear [groom],
>
> We'd like to take this opportunity on your wedding
> day to give you and your new bride our very best

wishes for your future life together. By the way, do
you wish to renew your subscription?

Yours sincerely,

Playboy magazine.'

Quotation or poem
Start to wrap up your speech with a quotation or a poem.
But keep it short. As best man, your speech will be the third
one of the day. Deliver an overlong poem and some of your
guests will nod off. Try not to use anything too sentimental.
There are hundreds of quotations and poems to choose
from (see pages 94–106 for a selection of quotations
and page 125 for further sources.)

Toast
Finish your speech with a toast (see pages 106–8 for some
examples). At this stage of the speeches everyone will be dying
to nip to the toilet or stretch their legs and then get to the bar.
Your toast will be a recognizable punctuation point. Always end
it with a simple phrase that everyone can repeat together, like
'The bride and groom!'

Chapter Nine

Writing the Speech

So, you have a basic structure to work to. Start composing your speech months, not days before the wedding. That's not to say it will take you months to write. It's likely you'll be able to sit down one evening and put all the salient points on paper (or preferably computer) within a couple of hours. If you do this early enough then you'll give yourself lots of time to add material, fine-tune your words and practise your delivery, resulting in a polished performance.

Speech length

Depending on the formality of the wedding, most best men's speeches run for between 7 and 12 minutes. If it's a 1,000-guest royal wedding you're best man for then you can make it longer; if it's family and a couple of friends in the village hall then you'd probably want to make it shorter. Check with the groom and the father of the bride as to how long they are planning to speak for. Your speech should be the longest of the three, but not by a disproportionate amount. You're not in an oratorical competition, you're communicating with friends.

Putting pen to paper

If possible, the best thing to do is to type your speech on a computer. That way you can amend and add to it over the weeks in the run-up to the wedding. Jot down the bare bones and then gradually flesh it out until you have it in full. This is when you need to make a decision as to how you're going to deliver your speech – are you going to read it word for word or use cue cards? (See pages 110 and 117).

If you're not confident that you can remember your speech just from notes or bullet points then you can always separate the fully written speech into small sections, print it out and then glue each section to a separate cue card. If you're going to read your speech this is the best way to prepare it as it avoids your holding several sheets of flimsy paper.

If you're going to deliver your speech using notes or bullet points you will need to have virtually memorized it (see page 110). When you have memorized it edit your speech document (keeping a copy of the original, just in case) so that you are left with the key points and the best lines. Make the type larger than you would for a normal letter or document. Print the bullet points out onto sheets of paper, cut them up and glue a few bullet points to each cue card. Number the cards, then punch a hole in the top left corner and group the cards together using a treasury tag. This way if you drop your cards you can pick them up and carry on rather than scrabbling around trying to get them back in order.

Great opening lines

They say that first impressions last. It's the same with speeches. Seasoned wedding-goers will tell you how important it is for the best man to get the guests on his side from the very start. To do this you need to open your speech with a killer opening line. It doesn't necessarily have to be hilarious and it doesn't have to be entirely original (none of those listed below are), but try to avoid clichés and jokes that may not appeal to everyone present.

'Apparently there are four crucial duties for a best man:

One: Help the groom get dressed. He really should know how to do that by now.

Two: Make sure he has a pee before he gets married. Look, I don't mind sending him to the toilet, but I'm not willing to check he actually has a pee.

Three: Ensure the groom's face and hair are in order. Well, if God couldn't get it right the first time then I've got no hope.

Finally: Make a speech to the bride and groom. Now, I was under the naive impression that this meant just the bride and groom. You know, maybe just us three in the vestry, having a chat and a cup of tea. So you can imagine how worried I was when I found out I actually had to do it in front of 100 people.'

[If the groom's paying for the wedding.] 'Typical. It's the first time [groom's] ever bought me dinner and I was so nervous about the speech that I couldn't eat it.'

'Ladies and gentlemen… the groom gave me a short list of topics I wasn't allowed to cover in the speech. [Remove a large wad of cue cards from your breast pocket and throw them away behind you.] There goes most of my speech then. Feel reassured now, [groom]?'

'Ladies and gentlemen. This is the moment you've all been waiting for. [Pause]. And there it goes.'

'I don't mind telling you I'm a little nervous. This isn't the first time today I've stood up from a warm seat with a piece of paper in my hand.'

'Unaccustomed as I am to pubic spanking… Oops!'

'I've just realized, while [father of the bride's] and [groom] were speaking before me, how much they have in common. After all, it's the first time in 25 years that [father of the bride] has been able to speak for more than five minutes without interruption from the women in his family, and it'll be the last time in 25 years that [groom] gets to do the same.'

'Over the years I've been like a mother to [groom]. I've watched him drink from the bottle; I've seen him stagger around stark naked; I've seen him trying to crawl; I've had to dress him. I've had to undress him. And God knows how many times I've cleaned up after him. I've even had to help him walk.'

'Fornication… Uh, sorry… [Say clearly and slowly] FOR AN OCCASION such as this I was dreading making the speech. That was until I found out exactly what I was supposed to say as best man. I discovered that once I'd hacksawed through [groom's] handcuffs the morning after the stag night, and once I'd handed [groom] the ring before today's service, all that was left was a five-minute speech in which I was to absolutely demolish [groom's] character. Never one to shun my duties, here goes…'

'Marriage is a wonderful thing. Marriage will teach [groom] loyalty, self-restraint and control. It will develop in him a sense of fair play and many other qualities he wouldn't need if he had stayed single.

[For best men who wear glasses] 'On the request of [groom], I have tried to memorize my speech. My memory's not as good as it used to be, so forgive me if I occasionally consult my notes. I did ask for an autocue, but apparently the wedding budget doesn't stretch that far. [Putting on glasses] Neither does my eyesight.'

'Ladies and gentlemen, I'm only going to speak for a couple of minutes because of my throat. If I go on too long, [bride] says she'll cut it.'

'If there's anybody here this afternoon who feels slightly nervous, it's probably because you just got married to [groom].'

'In making this speech I feel like one of Elizabeth Taylor's husbands. There have been so many before. The problem is how to make it interesting.'

'You know it's great to be at a normal wedding for once. Last week I went to a wedding where two aerials got married. The ceremony was dreadful, but the reception was great!'

'Six months ago when [groom] asked me to be his best man I decided to do a bit of research. All the books told me there are three crucial stages to the ceremony:

1 The aisle – it's the longest walk you'll ever take.

2 The altar – the place where two become one.

3 The hymn – a choral celebration of the marriage.

I think [bride] may have read the same books as me because as she took her place beside [groom] today, I swear I heard her whispering "Aisle Altar Hymn, Aisle Altar Hymn"'.

'I've really been looking forward to today. After all the years I've known him, [groom] has finally admitted that I am in fact the best man.'

'This is a very emotional day. Even I'm feeling a bit choked up. Mainly because I've had [groom's] hands around my neck, threatening to kill me if I mess up the speech.

Everything's so emotional. Look, even the cake is in tiers.'

'While travelling here I was wondering, as best man, how much I could drink without anyone noticing… [slurring] And I think that I have badly misjudged it.'

'I'd like to start this speech by introducing myself. [Best man], being a clever old chap, decided to dispense with the speech-making part of his best man's duties, and has employed the services of our company to take over from him.

Speeches R Us specialize in all those family occasions when a speech fits the bill: weddings, funerals, disciplining children in a patronizing manner – you get the gist. Anyway, we deliver a personally tailored speech for every occasion. Ask me afterwards for a brochure.'

'I couldn't help noticing that there's a bet on about the length of the best man's speech. Well, just to let you know, there might be a bit of insider dealing afoot. I placed a bet of an hour and a half. With the kitty currently at about £200 you might as well all settle back, make yourselves comfortable and enjoy the ride…'

'When he asked me to be his best man, you know, organize a stag weekend, get him to the church on time, and say a few nice words at the reception, I told [groom] it was a great honour to be asked, but that, quite frankly, I felt he'd be better off with someone else.

Then he offered me £50.

I said indignantly: "I'm not a man who can be bought!"

Then he offered me a £100…

Anyway, good afternoon, ladies and gentlemen. My name is [best man] and it's my pleasure to be [groom's] best man today.'

Subjects to avoid

There's nothing wrong with embarrassing the groom – he and all of the guests will expect you to do this – but you don't want to humiliate him. That's what the stag night was for. During the wedding speech you want your words to make him laugh and blush. Not cry and go green. If in doubt, leave it out.

DON'T MENTION ex-girlfriends. Everyone knows the groom has had past loves, but no one particularly wants to be reminded on his wedding day. Lurid tales of ex-paramours will just make the groom squirm in his seat. It will make the bride and both sets of parents extremely uncomfortable. And any ex-girlfriends who happen to be present among the guests (there's always one) will be mortified.

DON'T IMPLY that the groom is a womanizer. Even if he's spent the day with his hands all over the bridesmaids, don't even mention it. Have a stern word with him, yes. But don't tell everyone else.

DON'T MENTION divorce. One of the newly-weds may well be a divorcee. If they are then everyone will know. So don't bother reminding them. It will be seen to be in bad taste.

DON'T MENTION heavy drinking, drugs, gambling or fighting. These particular habits are very close to the bone. There will be other safer material about which you can mock the groom.

DON'T MENTION sexually transmitted diseases.

NEVER MAKE FUN of the bride. This area is for the father of the bride's speech, not yours. Even if the groom has chosen someone you certainly wouldn't say was beautiful, as far as you're concerned, today she is a paragon of pulchritude. Don't ever forget that.

AVOID racist or homophobic jokes. They're not funny and you'll just end up looking like an idiot.

AVOID sexist jokes. A little light banter about how the groom might end up being henpecked by his new wife is okay. But anything stronger won't go down well – half of your audience will be female.

DON'T MENTION arguments between the bride and groom. Even if they tend to fight like cat and dog, no one, least of all them, will want to be reminded on their wedding day. You're supposed to be celebrating the union between man and wife. Not disunion.

MOTHER-IN-LAW jokes are clichés. Think of something more original. Besides, if you mock her she may think the groom put you up to it. Also bear in mind that you may well encounter her again at future family events, such as christenings and anniversaries.

DON'T MAKE FUN of the bride's friends. She may suspect you and the groom have a conspiracy against her. You'll also halve your chances of having a drink bought for you afterwards.

DON'T EMBARRASS either set of parents, however tempting it may be, and never make jokes about the ceremony or the reception. You can bet your bottom dollar that the whole day cost the bride's father an arm and a leg. Besides, you're eating and drinking for free.

DIRTY ADULT JOKES are a no-no. Seaside postcard humour is okay, but anything stronger will get a mixed reception.

DON'T TALK ABOUT the performance of either bride or groom in bed. In any case, how would you know?

DON'T MENTION unemployment if either bride or groom have recently lost their job. You want people to think they stand a chance of a happy life together, don't you?

DON'T MENTION any psychological counselling either newly-wed might have undergone. Very few receptions have leather couches to lie on.

DON'T BRING UP past brushes with the law. Even if the groom is an ex-convict, no one will want reminding. Least of all the father of the bride.

Safe joke material

A best man's speech isn't complete until you make fun of the groom. It's difficult sometimes knowing what traits of his to mock. The following are generally considered safe territory: old school

How rude can your jokes be?

Don't assume that the grannies and grandpas at the wedding haven't heard rude jokes before. They were telling smutty stories before you were born. Having said that, the last thing you want to do, as best man, is offend anyone at the wedding. A light-hearted story about the wedding couple being caught in bed by the in-laws will amuse everyone, grannies included. But a graphic sexual description is pushing the envelope too far. You only have to hint at something sexual and everyone who is supposed to will know exactly what you mean. The only guests who won't are the underage ones and you don't want them to in any case. The golden rule is: if in doubt, leave it out.

The chief usher at my wedding has never forgotten a wedding he attended a few years ago. The parents of the bride were born-again Christians and were very proud to have secured the services of the local vicar who was delighted to be the one to marry the young couple.

After a very lengthy traditional Anglican service, everyone went straight from the church to the wedding reception which was being held, at great expense, at a stately manor house in the countryside. Once all the guests arrived, the receiving line was longer than a milkman's round. Best man and, as it happens, the vicar, were both dying for the toilet but quickly discovered there were no facilities until after they had queued up and been through the receiving line. Thinking no one would notice they both nipped around the side of the stately manor in the back garden. Fortunately no one spotted them.

When it came to the speeches, the best man thought he would regale all the guests, many of whom, like the bride's parents, were born-again Christians, with a story about how he and the vicar had been caught short together. When no one laughed he thought he'd go one step further and supply a few details about the size of the vicar's manhood. Well… if you thought the vicar was mortified, imagine what the bride's parents and their friends thought. The best man had misjudged the occasion. Some things are better left unsaid.

reports, lack of skill in the kitchen, lack of DIY skills, dress sense, table manners, poor physical fitness, vanity, slobbishness, singing skills, lack of culture, poor haircuts, embarrassing stories from childhood and school; driving test.

Ideas

People are expecting anecdotes and funny episodes about your relationship as best friend of the groom. Think back to when you first met him. Perhaps you were at the same school or college. Maybe you've both worked for the same company. You're bound to have played sport together, gone on holiday together and certainly gone out drinking together. All these adventures, however mundane, will provide a wealth of material.

You may even be able to include things that happened on the stag night (keep it clean); or you might add last minute details from earlier during the wedding day.

If you haven't known the groom for that long then why not quiz his family members beforehand for some funny episodes from his life? Ask about his childhood, his birthdays, his pets, his first car, family holidays, former jobs, and so on. Old school friends will be able to throw up some great little stories. What about asking his parents for an old school report? Read that out during the speech and you're guaranteed to get some laughs.

A friend of mine was at a wedding in the USA where the bride's uncle was asked to make a speech. Somehow the crafty old fellow managed to get hold of a teacher's report from when the bride was at junior high school. When it came to reading out her English lesson report the guests were in hysterics as the uncle relayed the terrible things that the teacher had written about his niece's lingual incompetence. Not surprisingly the bride was mortified with embarrassment, but it wasn't until after he'd finished the speech and she'd told him that her old English teacher was in fact one of the guests that he realized just how embarrassed she really was.

Once you start thinking about times and experiences you have shared together you'll find that you're able to jot down loads of amusing yarns from the groom's past. The more embarrassing (within reason), the better. People laugh at things they can identify with. There's little point telling a story about something no one in the audience will be able to relate to. But if it's a genuine story that really happened and you think it's funny, then it probably will be funny for everyone else. The more details you include, the more genuine and therefore amusing it will seem. Then again, don't be afraid to embellish or exaggerate where you see fit.

Although it's the job of the father of the bride to tell stories about his daughter, you may want to include the odd anecdote about the bride and groom as a couple.

Your speech isn't just about taking the mickey out of the groom, however. You should think of some heartfelt and poignant material, too. Perhaps something that proves what a great friend he is and what a good husband he will make.

Quotations

Many orators like to include a couple of choice quotations in their speech. Why not? As long as you don't use more than a couple and provided they are appropriate and you can link them into the speech, then they can make a worthy addition. They may even, if you're lucky, make you sound learned. A few examples follow. (See page 125 for sources of further quotes and poems.)

Marriage

'Marriage is the highest state of friendship. If happy it lessens our cares by dividing them, at the same time that it doubles our pleasures by mutual participation.'

Samuel Richardson
English writer and printer

'Marriage is our last, best chance to grow up.'

Joseph Barth
Maltese ophthalmologist

'"Marriage". This I call the will that moves two to create the one which is more than those who created it.'

Friedrich Nietzsche
German philosopher and poet

_____

'A princely marriage is the brilliant edition of a universal fact, and as such it rivets mankind.'

Walter Bagehot
English banker and essayist

_____

'A successful marriage is an edifice that must be rebuilt every day.'

Andre Maurois
French author

_____

'All married couples should learn the art of battle as they should learn the art of making love. Good battle is objective and honest – never vicious or cruel. Good battle is healthy and constructive, and brings to a marriage the principle of equal partnership.'

Ann Landers
American columnist

_____

'I used to believe that marriage would diminish me, reduce my options. That you had to be someone less to live with someone else when, of course, you have to be someone more.'

Candice Bergen
American actress

_____

'That is what marriage really means: helping one another to reach the full status of being persons, responsible and autonomous beings who do not run away from life.'

Paul Tournier
Swiss physician and writer

'Marriage is the union of disparate elements. Male and female. Yin and yang. Proton and electron. What are we talking about here? Nothing less than the very tension that binds the universe. You see, when we look at marriage, people, we're looking at creation itself. "I am the sky," says the Hindu bridegroom to the bride. "You are the earth. We are sky and earth united.... You are my husband. You are my wife. My feet shall run because of you. My feet shall dance because of you. My heart shall beat because of you. My eyes see because of you. My mind thinks because of you and I shall love because of you."'

Diane Frolov and Andrew Schneider,
Northern Exposure

'Marriage. It's a hard term to define. Especially for me – I've ducked it like root canal. Still there's no denying the fact that marriage ranks right up there with birth and death as one of the three biggies in the human safari. It's the only one, though, that we'll celebrate with a conscious awareness. Very few of you remember your arrival and even fewer of you will attend your own funeral.'

Diane Frolov and Andrew Schneider,
Northern Exposure

'Nearly all marriages, even happy ones, are mistakes: in the sense that almost certainly (in a more perfect world, or even with a little more care in this very imperfect one) both partners might be found more suitable mates. But the real soul mate is the one you are actually married to.'

J. R. R. Tolkien
English author and poet

───────────────

'Intimacy is what makes a marriage. Not a ceremony, not a piece of paper from the state.'

Kathleen Norris
American poet and essayist

───────────────

'A successful marriage requires falling in love many times, always with the same person.'

Mignon McLaughlin
American journalist

───────────────

'A good marriage is one which allows for change and growth in the individuals and in the way they express their love.'

Pearl Buck
American author

───────────────

'I love being married. It's so great to find that one special person you want to annoy for the rest of your life.'

Rita Rudner
American comedienne

'For it is mutual trust, even more than mutual interest that holds human associations together. Our friends seldom profit us but they make us feel safe…
Marriage is a scheme to accomplish exactly that same end.'

H. L. Mencken
American writer and satirist

––––––––––––––––

'Never marry but for love; but see that thou lovest what is lovely.'

William Penn
English philosopher

––––––––––––––––

'A good marriage is like a good trade: each thinks he got the better deal.'

Ivern Ball
Unknown master of quotations

––––––––––––––––

'After seven years of marriage, I'm sure of two things – first, never wallpaper together, and second, you'll need two bathrooms… both for her. The rest is a mystery, but a mystery I love to be involved in.'

Dennis Miller
American comedian

––––––––––––––––

'Marriage is like a pair of shears. Oft times working in opposite directions, but punishing anyone that comes between them.'

Sydney Smith
English writer and cleric

'An occasional lucky guess as to what makes a wife tick is the best a man can hope for. Even then, no sooner has he learned how to cope with the tick than she tocks.'

Ogden Nash
American poet

'Chains do not hold a marriage together. It is threads, hundreds of tiny threads which sew people together through the years. That is what makes a marriage last – more than passion or even sex!'

Simone Signoret
French actress

'I would say that the surest measure of a man's or a woman's maturity is the harmony, style, joy and dignity he creates in his marriage, and the pleasure and inspiration he provides for his spouse.'

Benjamin Spock
American pediatrician

'Marriage – as its veterans know well – is the continuous process of getting used to things you hadn't expected.'

Tom Mullen
American columnist

'Car manufacturer's formula for a successful marriage: Stick to one model!

Unknown

'The more you invest in a marriage, the more valuable
it becomes.'

Amy Grant
American songwriter

––––––––––

'In marriage, each partner is to be an encourager
rather than a critic, a forgiver rather than a collector
of hurts, an enabler rather than a reformer.'

H. Norman Wright and Gary J. Oliver
American theologians

––––––––––

'I pay very little regard… to what a young person
says on the subject of marriage. If they profess
a disinclination for it, I only set it down that they
haven't seen the right person yet.'

Jane Austen
English author

––––––––––

Love

'All thoughts, all passions, all delights.
Whatever stirs this mortal frame.
All are but ministers of love
And feed His sacred flame.'

Samuel Taylor Coleridge
English poet

––––––––––

'The meeting of two personalities is like the contact of two chemical substances: if there is any reaction, both are transformed.'

Carl Jung
Swiss psychiatrist and thinker

'To love and be loved is to feel the sun from both sides.'

David Viscott
American psychiatrist

'Love is the immortal flow of energy that nourishes, extends and preserves. Its eternal goal is life.

Smiley Blanton
American psychoanalyst

'A relationship is like a rose,
How long it lasts, no one knows;
Love can erase an awful past,
Love can be yours, you'll see at last;
To feel that love, it makes you sigh,
To have it leave, you'd rather die;
You hope you've found that special rose,
'Cause you love and care for the one you chose.'

Rob Cella
American writer

'Woe to the man whose heart has not learned while young to hope, to love – and to put its trust in life.

Joseph Conrad
Polish-born English novelist

'We are all born for love. It is the principle of existence, and its only end.'

Benjamin Disraeli
British politician and author

'You will find as you look back upon your life that the moments when you have truly lived are the moments when you have done things in the spirit of love.'

Henry Drummond
Canadian poet

'Immature love says: "I love you because I need you." Mature love says: "I need you because I love you."'

Erich Fromm
German–American psychologist

'In love the paradox occurs that two beings become one and yet remain two.'

Erich Fromm
German–American psychologist

'The moment you have in your heart this extraordinary thing called love and feel the depth, the delight, the ecstasy of it, you will discover that for you the world is transformed.'

J. Krishnamurti
Indian thinker and teacher

'Treasure the love you receive above all. It will survive long after your good health has vanished.'

Og Mandino
American author

'To love deeply in one direction makes us more loving in all others.'

Anne Sophie Swetchine
Russian mystic

'Perhaps the feelings that we experience when we are in love represent a normal state. Being in love shows a person who he should be.'

Anton Chekhov
Russian writer and physician

'All love that has not friendship for its base, is like a mansion built upon sand.'

Ella Wheeler Wilcox
American author and poet

'To be brave is to love someone unconditionally, without expecting anything in return. To just give. That takes courage, because we don't want to fall on our faces or leave ourselves open to hurt.'

Madonna
American singer–songwriter

'Love is everything it's cracked up to be... It really is worth fighting for, being brave for, risking everything for.'

Erica Jong
American author

'There is always some madness in love. But there is also always some reason in madness.'

Friedrich Nietzsche
German philosopher and poet

'What else is love but understanding and rejoicing in the fact that another person lives, acts, and experiences otherwise than we do...?'

Friedrich Nietzsche
German philosopher and poet

'There is no remedy for love but to love more.'

Henry David Thoreau
American author and poet

'Love is the difficult realization that something other than oneself is real.'

Iris Murdoch
English author

'To love is to receive a glimpse of heaven.'

Karen Sunde
American playwright

'Age does not protect you from love. But love,
to some extent, protects you from age.'

Jeanne Moreau
French actress and director

'Real love is a permanently self-enlarging experience.'

M. Scott Peck
American author

'Love is an act of endless forgiveness, a tender look
which becomes a habit.'

Peter Ustinov
English actor and writer

'For one human being to love another; that is
perhaps the most difficult of all our tasks, the
ultimate, the last test and proof, the work for
which all other work is but preparation.'

Rainer Maria Rilke
Austrian poet

'He who is in love is wise and is becoming wiser,
sees newly every time he looks at the object beloved,
drawing from it with his eyes and his mind those
virtues which it possesses.'

Ralph Waldo Emerson
American essayist and poet

'Love is an exploding cigar we willingly smoke.'

Lynda Barry
American writer and cartoonist

'One word frees us of all the weight and pain of life:
That word is love.'

Sophocles
Greek playwright

The toast

In theory, the best man is not officially expected to make a toast at the end of his speech. The father of the bride will have toasted the happy couple and the groom will have toasted the bridesmaids. But in practice, if you want to toast the bride and groom again at the end of your speech, then why not?

The toast should always come at the very end. So as not to spring it on the guests unawares, always give them a few moments' notice to charge their glasses before you raise your own. You should have put aside a glass of bubbly near you at the beginning of your speech in readiness. Once everyone has had a chance to refill theirs, raise your glass in the air and propose a toast. Below are a few toast suggestions. Always finish off the toast with the words: 'To the bride and groom.'

'My greatest wish for the two of you is that through the years your love for each other will grow so much that years from now you will look back on this day, your wedding day, as the day you loved each other the least.'

'May the best day of your past be the worst day of your future.'

'Here's to the groom, a man who keeps his head though he loses his heart.'

'May the roof above you never fall in and may you both never fall out.'

'To the lamp of love – may it burn brightest in the darkest hours and never flicker in the winds of trial.'

'May "for better or worse" be far better than worse.'

'The man or woman you really love will never grow old to you. Through the wrinkles of time, through the bowed frame of years, you will always see the dear face and feel the warm heart union of your eternal love.'

'May you have many children and may they grow mature in taste and healthy in colour and as sought after as the contents of the glass.'

'Let us toast the health of the bride. Let us toast the health of the groom. Let us toast the person that tied. Let us toast every guest in the room.'

'Happy marriages begin when we marry the one we love, and they blossom when we love the one we married.'

'There is nothing nobler or more admirable than when two people who see eye to eye keep house as man and wife, confounding their enemies and delighting their friends.'

'Here's to the groom with bride so fair, and here's to the bride with groom so rare.'

'Coming together is a beginning; keeping together is progress; working together is success.'

'Long life and happiness – for your long life will be my happiness.'

'Seek a happy marriage with wholeness of heart, but do not expect to reach the promised land without going through some wilderness together.'

'May you live as long as you like, and have all you like as long as you live.'

'To the bridegroom: He is leaving us for a better life. But we are not leaving him.'

'To the bride: May she share everything with her husband, including the housework.'

'To the bride and groom: As you slide down the banister of life, may the splinters never face the wrong way!'

'To the bride and groom: I wish you health, I wish you happiness, I wish you wealth, I wish you heaven – what more could I wish?'

Chapter Ten

Speech Delivery

The manner in which you deliver your speech is just as important as the content. Make sure you watch presenters or newsreaders on television. Think how great orators and stand-up comics perform to their audiences. They all deliver their words in different ways, but there's one thing they all share: stage presence. Those with the greatest stage presence are probably born with it. But it is a skill you can learn, too. The following tips will imbue even the most jittery of public performers with the confidence required. Armed with the right technique, even a nervous wreck can pass off as something of a rhetorician.

Practising

All the best speeches are rehearsed several times. Whether you're a politician, a stand-up comic or a best man you need to practise, practise and practise. And then practise a bit more. This will help you appear confident and ensure that your words flow smoothly.

If you partially memorize your speech then you'll be able to use cue cards rather than a fully written script – which will of course appear and sound a lot better and will allow you to look up at the guests as you speak. It's important to engage your audience.

Once you have all your brilliant words down on paper, there are then several ways to rehearse your speech:

Film yourself with a camcorder. This will give you a picture perfect idea of how you might look on the day – you can even dress up in your suit if you want to make it really authentic.

A friend of mine did this and said he was so impressed by how professional he looked that on the actual day he was fearless and his speech went like clockwork.

When you play back the film you should pay attention to your stance, enunciation, gestures, pace and overall delivery. Make notes on things to work on and see if you can improve on subsequent practice runs.

If you don't own a camcorder then borrow or hire one. (Even an audio recording is better than nothing.) I cannot stress how much you will gain in confidence each time you film yourself and see yourself improving.

Make your speech in front of a mirror. Again, if you like you can dress up in your suit and make your rehearsal realistic. Use a full-length mirror so you can analyse your gestures and stance. Since you'll be trying to watch your reflection, this technique will train you to look up towards the audience as much as possible.

Practise your speech in front of a close friend. Preferably choose someone who will give you an honest opinion and who isn't attending the wedding – otherwise they won't laugh at your jokes the second time round.

If they're not close to the wedding party they'll spot inappropriate material in the speech that you may have overlooked. An outsider's opinion on your delivery and presentation is very important too.

Don't give in to nerves

Every best man gets nervous about his speech. Even the most experienced and assured public speakers will admit that behind their confident exterior they are sometimes a complete bag of nerves. But a bit of anxiety is good. It is nature's way of making sure that we perform well under pressure. What you must try to do is transform your nervousness from negative energy into positive energy. With a lot of preparation and practise this is easily done.

First of all make sure you have run through your speech at least five times (see Practising, opposite).

I have a friend who is regularly asked to make speeches at weddings and public engagements. He has a special method of preparation which may sound strange but is in fact extremely effective: he places his speech script in the bathroom and every time he goes in there he quickly reads it through. It doesn't take long before he knows his words inside out.

Before the wedding ceremony starts and everyone gets embroiled in their various duties, make sure you agree with the other speakers what order the speeches are to run in. Traditionally it's the father of the bride who kicks off proceedings. He is followed by the groom and then the best man. If you're nervous, the last thing you want to happen is that, during the reception dinner, just as you are tucking into your dessert, the father of the bride taps you on the shoulder and says: 'Right, you're speaking in 30 seconds!'

Most wedding speeches take place at the end of the reception dinner. It's a good idea to pay a quick visit to the toilet five minutes before the speeches are due to start. You can check yourself in the mirror, remove any spinach from your teeth and ensure that you won't be desperate for the toilet by the time your turn comes.

A best man, in particular, may have to wait up to 45 minutes for the father of the bride and the groom to finish their speeches before it's his turn to speak – you'd be considered very rude if you rushed off for a toilet break during their speeches.

For the vast majority of best men, the most nervous moment of their whole day is the few scary minutes just before they have to get up and speak. This is normally just as the groom is winding up his own speech. For the most nervous people it can feel like they're about to face an executioner. Take a few seconds to analyse the mood of the guests around you. They will be looking forward to your speech. They are on your side. They want you to do well and they want to laugh at your jokes. What can possibly go wrong? Even if you stumble over your lines, the guests will be polite enough to overlook it.

Many professional speakers perform a quick set of exercises just before they stand up to speak. In a wedding situation, as best man, you will perhaps be seated at the top table. You can't exactly step outside the reception venue during the groom's speech to ready yourself, but there are a few relaxation exercises you can do in your seat to get your mind and body ready for your big moment.

Sit upright with your arms by your sides and your feet flat on the floor. Take a deep breath through your nose and at the same time clench your fists, push your feet onto the ground and hunch up your shoulders. (Everyone will be looking at the groom at this stage, so don't worry too much what you look like.) Hold your position for a few seconds and then slowly breathe out while loosening your shoulders, fists and feet. Feel all your nervousness and stress evaporate. Continue breathing slowly and deeply until it's your turn to stand up and speak.

Just before you open your mouth for your great opening line, there's a psychological trick you can use to inspire yourself with confidence. Instead of pondering on your own nervousness, think instead about something happy or funny. Perhaps think back to the last great joke you told your friends down the pub, or a funny incident involving a member of your family. As you do this you won't be able to stop yourself from smiling, at least inwardly, and at the same time all your spirits will be lifted and the negative energy of your nervousness will disappear. Your face will relax, the guests will notice how comfortable you look and you'll be able to launch your speech with a confident and easy start.

These first few words are the trickiest bit. Once you've got through your introduction and made them laugh then, provided you've done your preparation, the rest of the speech should be plain sailing.

Don't be overawed by the size of your audience. Believe it or not, there is actually a benefit to having a large number of guests: your jokes don't have to be that funny. If you only get a little titter from each guest, but there are 150 people present, then it will sound like loud laughing. You will hear this laughter from all around the room and automatically be filled with confidence. Laughter is a great antidote for nerves.

It's so important to think positively about your speech in the hours running up to the reception. Believe in yourself and be confident that you are going to deliver a wonderful address. Don't dwell on negative aspects, but instead think about how the guests are going to enjoy and laugh at your words, and how proud of you the bride and groom are going to be. Again, it's a psychological trick, but it's true that if you are able to envisage your speech being successful and being received well, then it's highly likely it will be.

Delivery and presentation

Nervousness has a fairly unpleasant way of manifesting itself: shaky hands, dry mouth and sweaty palms and brow on the one hand and, in extreme cases, feelings of nausea and loss of consciousness. Fortunately most of these physical signs (bar the last one) won't even be noticed by most of the guests. In any case, there are certain things you can do to hide them. Shaky hands are less noticeable if you use cue cards rather than large sheets of paper that will flap about. If you think you might suffer from dry mouth, then keep a glass of water near you during your speech and sip from it regularly. To avoid stammering, speak slowly and methodically – your speech will sound much better at this pace anyway. While a hot summer's day is perfect for a wedding, it's not ideal for a speaker who has to stand up in front of 150 people in a heavy formal suit. Just before you get up to make your speech, mop your brow and top lip with a handkerchief. Once you've got through the first few lines of your speech and everything is going well, your nervousness will disappear anyway and hopefully so will your perspiration.

Engage your audience

Try to get the guests on your side from the very start. This isn't difficult to do since they all want you to perform well anyway. As you stand up to speak, try to pick out three friendly faces in the crowd – one on the left, one in the middle and one on the right. They can either be people you know or just guests who look friendly. Throughout your speech you can keep coming back to these faces. You'll find their smiles will help maintain your confidence.

Provided your jokes are vaguely funny you'll find it easy to get the audience on your side. Fortunately the best man is usually the third person to speak at a wedding, so the guests will already be well warmed up before it's your turn. Even if you feel your words aren't that funny, there are other sure-fire ways to get the guests on your side. Ask them questions which you know will elicit a positive response: 'Doesn't the bride look absolutely gorgeous?'; 'Isn't the groom the luckiest man in the world?'; 'Isn't this the most wonderful wedding reception?' Even the most cynical of wedding guests will have to greet these questions with a rousing cheer. The more positive and vociferous their response, the more confident you will feel about the rest of your speech.

Another way to engage the guests is to include some of them in an interactive joke you play on the groom. An old favourite is the key trick. Before the wedding, buy 15 blank keys from a key cutter. At the start of the reception hand out the keys to various female guests. Tell each one to keep the key in her pocket during the speeches, but also make them promise to keep quiet about your little trick. During your speech announce something along the lines of the following: 'The bride is well aware that her husband has had quite a few girlfriends over the years. Now that he is happily married she is willing to overlook any past romances. But she would be very grateful if any ex-girlfriends here would kindly hand her any keys they may still have to her husband's flat.' At this point all 15 of the women should walk up to the bride and groom's table, and with a sheepish "sorry" hand her key to the bride. The stunt is even funnier if you can get some heavily pregnant women or even a granny to participate too.

Pace and projection

Many speakers, especially the nervous ones, have a tendency to rush through their speech, as if it's an ordeal they want to get through as quickly as possible. Remember that a slow, deliberate address sounds far better than a hurried one. You should practise speaking slowly and clearly. If you listen to professional speakers you'll notice that they leave gaps between their sentences and pause before and after crucial phrases. It makes the words sound more heartfelt. Speak too rapidly and the guests may miss some of your choice words.

You don't have to shout, especially if you have a microphone. But you do have to enunciate each word and try to project it to the very back of the room or marquee. You can achieve this by articulating your mouth more than you would normally and by not tailing off at the end of your sentences. Imagine that you are speaking just for the benefit of the guests sitting at the very back of the room. Whenever I speak publicly, near the beginning of my speech I always check by picking out a group at the back and asking them if they can hear properly. If they can then you can rest assured that everyone else can too.

How to use a mic

Acquaint yourself fully with how the microphone works before you use it. At the beginning of the wedding reception it's a good idea to approach whoever is in charge of the sound (normally the DJ) and get him or her to show you how to adjust the stand and switch the device on. You don't want to be one of those poor speakers who finds himself tapping the head of the microphone and looking around cluelessly asking 'is this thing turned on?' It's never a great way to start any speech.

However confident you are in the strength of your speaking voice, don't decline to use a microphone if one's available. Even very strong speakers tend to tail away at the end of sentences. A mic will ensure that older guests with hearing aids (there's always at least one) and those at the very back hear every word you say.

I was at the wedding of one of my best friends recently where the microphone kept playing up. Every few minutes it would screech with feedback. Two of the speakers chose to use it, nonetheless, while the best man decided to give it a miss. But the reception was in a large hall and there was noisy traffic passing by outside, so even with all the feedback, the amplified speeches were much better received than the non-amplified one. Guests at the back of the room barely heard a word the best man said.

For maximum effect, your mouth should be about 20 centimetres (9 inches) away from the mic when you speak into it – that's just longer than the distance between your little finger and your thumb when you stretch out your hand. If you don't have a microphone stand, but just a hand-held mic, try not to wave it around as you speak or much of what you say will be lost. This is something you can practise in front of a mirror with a hairbrush when rehearsing your best man's speech.

Stance

The way you stand will have a massive effect on how you deliver your speech and how well it is received. For the guests, your stance will be the most obvious part of your body language. Try to stand upright with your arms down by your sides and your palms open to the audience. This will give the impression that you are confident, open and friendly. Avoid crossing your arms – which looks defensive – and keep your hands out of your pockets – which looks too casual. Place your feet shoulder-width apart with one foot very slightly in front of the other. Shift your bodyweight slightly forward so that you are on the balls of your feet. This will give your speech much more vigour than if you stand back on your heels.

If the microphone is on a stand, place it slightly to the side of your body so that you don't look like you're hiding behind it. Whatever you do, don't lean on it or grasp it like a rock star.

Avoid making a speech from behind a table. Try to move so that there are no obstacles between you and your audience. Some reception venues and marquees can be fairly cramped. You may find that speaking from behind a table is your only option. If this is the case then whatever you do, don't lean on the table – it looks aggressive and will put off the guests.

You could always move to another vantage point halfway through your speech. Some guests may not have an ideal view, or there may be pillars in the way. There's nothing to stop you facing one way for the first half of the speech and then moving your position slightly for the second half.

I remember a huge wedding I attended in France a few years ago. At the reception there were so many guests that when they sat down to dinner they filled two separate rooms. Fortunately people sitting in the smaller room were able to follow the speakers via a video link. But at one point the best man, using a portable microphone, walked from the first room and spoke for a while directly to the guests in the second room. He looked very confident and all the guests appreciated the extra effort.

Notes and cue cards

A lot of orators choose to write their speech out verbatim on a script. If you're not a very confident speaker then this is probably a good idea, but it looks much more professional if you try to memorize most of your words and then put key phrases on small cue cards. Sheets of paper tend to flap around while you're speaking, especially if nerves have rendered your hands a bit shaky. Cue cards, on the other hand, are much less flimsy. Ideally you want to be able to lift your head so that you're looking at your audience as much as you can. Reading verbatim won't allow you to do this, but occasionally referring to cue cards as prompting devices will (see page 85).

I remember watching a film of the first speech I ever made. Because I hadn't bothered to learn my words at all, I was forced to read it out from a sheet of paper word for word. It turned out that I only looked up at my audience three times during the whole speech – once at the beginning, once after I got a particularly loud laugh in the middle, and once at the end. The rest of the time I had my face buried in my script which looked awful. Even if you do have to read out your speech word for word, pause and look up at the guests as often as you can without losing your place. It makes such a noticeable difference.

Gestures and movements

No one wants to hear a speech delivered by a motionless waxwork dummy. But at the same time it can be very irritating if the speaker moves around and waves his arms about. You want to be animated but controlled.

A lot of nervous public speakers have annoying little habits they are completely unaware of. They jiggle coins in their pocket, play with their hair, cover their mouth, rustle their notes, sway from side to side, rock backwards and forwards, shuffle their feet, scratch their nose, pull their ear, or fiddle with jewellery or glasses.

At first it may be endearing, but after a short while your listeners will find it irritating to watch. If you get a chance to film your speech during practice you may be able to eliminate these distracting movements and gestures.

Props

The right props can work wonders, while the wrong ones can be a disaster. Years ago I went to a beautiful church wedding where the family of both the groom and the bride were very religious indeed. The bride's parents were especially pious – so much so that as far as they knew their daughter hadn't yet shared a bed with the groom.

The best man, bless him, thought he would regale the guests with a bit of light-hearted banter about premarital sex. Halfway through the speech he produced a sports bag from under the table and proceeded to remove several (what he thought were amusing) props to illustrate his story. Imagine the bride and groom's horror when he brandished a set of handcuffs, a packet of condoms and a couple of pornographic magazines. Instead of the guffaws of laughter that the best man was expecting, there was stunned silence. The props immediately went straight back in the bag and the best man quickly and sheepishly hurried through to the end of his speech.

In order to achieve the desired effect the props have to be the correct props. I've seen speeches where the best man has used a projector to display photos of the groom when he was a baby. I've seen speeches where the father of the bride has revealed a security blanket that the bride had been inseparable from when she was a toddler. I've seen speeches where the best man has played a recording of the groom singing a solo on a drunken night out. All three occasions were received with good humour.

Think long and hard about the props before you incorporate them into your speech. And always remember: electrical props such as CD players and projectors can, and often do, malfunction or go missing just when you need them.

Be conversational

Just because you've spent weeks working out the funny and heartfelt words you plan to use in your speech, this doesn't mean that you need to deliver them in an especially formal or stilted manner. Try to be conversational. That's not to say that slang and swear words should litter your speech. Hopefully your words will be considered and imaginative, but the style that you deliver them in should be the same as the style of a normal, everyday conversation with a nod towards the formality of the occasion.

In times past wedding speeches were far more reserved and ceremonial than they are today. Granted, if you've been asked to speak at a state or royal wedding then your words should reflect the formality of the event. But at most of the weddings we mere mortals are invited to, we are among close friends. A certain respectful familiarity will be expected.

Try not to sound affected. Be relaxed and chatty when you speak. Don't put on airs and graces. If you have a strong regional accent then be yourself and use that accent to great effect. No one's expecting you to sound like the Queen. If you put on an act everyone will think you're being fake and insincere.

Years ago I attended a wedding in Oxford where the social backgrounds of the bride's and groom's family couldn't have been more dissimilar. The bride came from a very well-heeled, almost aristocratic family, while the groom was working class and proud of it. It turns out his best man wasn't so proud of it. You could tell that he had a strong Newcastle accent, yet he tried to disguise it by talking in a fake posh accent. No one was impressed, least of all the bride, and he ended up sounding like a buffoon.

Vocal variety – don't be monotonous

Even if the content is enthralling and witty, a speech delivered in the same dull, flat monotone can be the most excruciating thing to listen to. A bit of vocal variety will liven things up for the guests. Vary the pace, pitch and volume of your delivery to emphasize certain words. If you're quoting someone you may wish to impersonate their voice or speak louder at key moments, especially for the toast. Some anecdotes may sound better if you recount them quickly, while others may benefit from a slower delivery. The key thing is not to gabble or mumble incoherently.

Next time you hear a speech listen to how the speaker varies the way he speaks. Pay attention to the way television and radio presenters deliver their lines and how they pace what they are saying and change their tone of voice. The more you're able to do this the more likely you are to keep your audience interested (and awake).

Dealing with interruptions and hecklers

Don't worry. You're not a stand-up comedian. If anyone interrupts your speech or heckles you it's probably just to encourage you or get a laugh. It can be very distracting, however, and put you off your stride. For the nervous speaker it can spell disaster. There are several failsafe ways to deal with interruptions. Don't get too involved with hecklers. Simply look across to them, nod in acknowledgement, say 'Thank you very much for that' and carry on with your speech. You may even wish to acknowledge them by name (it's highly unlikely you'll get heckled by a complete stranger at a wedding) so that they get the attention they're obviously craving. Whatever you do, don't get into a debate with them otherwise you'll lose your train of thought and the whole momentum of the speech.

You may feel like defending yourself from hecklers and giving them some backchat, a bit like stand-up comics do. But remember, stand-up comics are quick-witted professional performers. If you, as an amateur, start trying to score points with hecklers it could backfire and get very uncomfortable indeed.

Above all, relax. Best men always tend to get too worked up about their speech. So what if you don't sound like a professional? So what if you don't make everyone split their sides with laughter? As long as you make an effort, sound sincere and engage your audience, everyone will love you.

Useful Sources

Websites

There are thousands of wedding and wedding-related websites out there covering every possible aspect of the big day.

General

www.bridesbook.co.uk
www.confetti.co.uk
www.hitched.co.uk
www.our-wedding-plans.co.uk
www.theweddingguide.co.uk

Stag celebrations

www.activepursuits.com
A one-stop directory for activities throughout the UK.

www.adventure001.com
Offer activities such as flying, driving, shooting and ballooning throughout the UK.

www.brillianttrips.co.uk
Organize stag weekends throughout the UK and Europe.

www.chillisauce.co.uk
Offer stag nights and weekends throughout the UK.

www.clubclassbus.com
Pick up the stag party, queue jump into the best bars and nightclubs. Available in Edinburgh, Glasgow, Newcastle, London, Bristol and Manchester.

www.crocodileevents.co.uk
Organize stag weekends throughout the UK.

www.eclipseleisure.co.uk
Organize stag nights and weekends throughout the UK and Europe.

www.expedia.co.uk
> Although not a specialist 'stag' website, you can book travel, activities, sports tickets, etc.

www.freedomltd.com/stag-weekends
> Offer day activities, stag nights and weekends, mainly in the UK.

www.greatescapades.co.uk
> Stag weekends throughout the UK, and in Prague, Dublin, Amsterdam and Barcelona.

www.the stagdo.com
> Organize stag weekends in Nottingham, Cardiff, Bournemouth and Bristol.

www.callofthewild.co.uk/stag-dos-how-to-plan-them
> Offer stag nights, weekends – single and multi-activity.

www.lastminute.com
> Again, although not a specialist 'stag' website, you can book travel, activities, sports tickets, etc.

www.lastnightoffreedom.com
> Offer stag weekends in UK and Europe, along with customised T-shirts, etc.

www.maximise.co.uk
> Activities and adventure sports and offer stag weekend packages.

www.murder-mystery-events.com
> Murder mystery parties in a 'Carry On Agatha Christie style'. Offer stag night packages.

www.nationalkarting.co.uk
> Lists indoor and outdoor karting circuits.

www.organise-events.co.uk
> Offer stag weekends in the UK and Europe.

www.pt-yachtcharters.com/stag_hen.htm
> Experience sailing or powerboating followed by a party night.

www.redsevenleisure.co.uk
> Organize stag nights and weekends, both in the UK and abroad.

www.releasetravel.co.uk
Offer over 27 destinations in the UK and abroad for stag weekends.

www.stagweb.co.uk
Organize stag weekends, stag parties and stag nights.

www.stagweekends.co.uk
Stag weekend packages in the UK, plus Tallinn and Prague.

www.ultimatedayout.com
Organize activity days – sailing, power boats, racing cards and track days.

www.ukpsf.com
The United Kingdom Paintball Sports Federation – lists paintballing sites throughout the UK.

www.whackysports.com
Offer activity days for stag parties.

Limousine hire

www.callalimo.co.uk
www.carsforstars-nationwide.co.uk
www.limohiredirectory.com
www.limoinlondon.co.uk
www.limoshop.co.uk
www.whatlimouk.com

Party accessories and fancy dress

www.dressingupboxonline.co.uk
www.forevermemories.co.uk
www.partybox.co.uk
www.staggerin.com
www.the-joke-shop.com
www.thepartyplacemailorder.co.uk
www.ukballoondecorators.com

Customised T-shirts

www.shirtinator.co.uk
www.clothes2order.com
wwwstreetshirts.co.uk
www.tshirtstudio.com
www.zikzak.co.uk

Wedding car decorations

www.confetti.co.uk/shopping
www.weddingwonderland.net

Sources of quotes for speech

www.comedy-zone.net/guide/quotes.htm
www.famousquotes.me.uk
www.quotations.co.uk
www.quotationspage.com
www.quotegarden.com

Speech courses

www.instantspeakingsuccess.com
www.speakfirst.co.uk
www.professionalspeakers.biz
www.public-speaking.org
www.the-asc.org.uk

Books

De Vicq DeCumptich, Roberto; *Love Quotes* (HarperCollins Australia, 1996)

Lansky, Bruce (Editor); *For Better or for Worse: Best Quotes about Marriage* (Meadowbrook Press, 1995)

Metcalf, Fred (Compiler); Scully, Mike (Introduction); *The Penguin Dictionary of Modern Humorous Quotations* (Penguin Books, 2002)

Sherrin, Ned; *The Oxford Dictionary of Humorous Quotations* (Oxford University Press 2012)

The Hutchinson Pocket Love and Marriage Quotes (Hutchinson Pocket Series, Helicon, 1995)

Knowles, Elizabeth; *The Oxford Dictionary of Quotations* (Oxford University Press 2004)

Acknowledgements

www.quotationspage.com
www.worldweddingtraditions.com

Index